PRAISE

In *Water Mask*, Monica Devine explores the unmapped edges of the human spirit with the same poet's eye that she uses to describe her raw encounters with the natural world. Her keen awareness is a gift to readers as we sink deep into the landscape and culture that is Alaska. In these finely crafted vignettes, we feel the joyful humor of a Native women's doll-making circle, experience the cycle of life through the harvest of salmon, and ponder the nature of fear when the waves of stormy seas bring her trembling to her knees. This is a book to be savored, the way one might sip the first rays of sunshine cresting the peaks of the Chugach Range.

—KAYLENE JOHNSON-SULLIVAN, author of *Canyons and Ice* and *Our Perfect Wild*

Picture Alaska—her braided rivers and Arctic tundra, her tidal shorelines and thrashing salmon. Imagine flying over the Yukon-Kuskokwim Delta with an inexperienced pilot, charging into an ever-changing rodeo of sky, clouds so thick it's like flying through milk. Imagine Yup'ik elders whose humble behavior and reverence for their homeland teaches you more about living with intention than formal education ever could. Imagine learning that to practice deep listening is to practice silence. Imagine spending 21 days on a 42-foot trawler boating the Inside Passage. Monica Devine's new collection, *Water Mask*, captures these experiences alongside stories of New Mexico deserts, Wyoming horses, and family, making accessible through lyrical essays this remarkable American landscape.

—PAGE LAMBERT, author of *In Search of Kinship* and *Shifting Stars*

WATER MASK

WATER MASK

MONICA DEVINE

University of Alaska Press

Fairbanks

Published by
University of Alaska Press
P.O. Box 756240
Fairbanks, AK 99775-6240

Cover design by UA Press.
Interior design by 590 design.

www.monicadevine.com

Cover art by Dominique Fortin.

Thanks to the late Jim Harrison for permission to print "Cabin Poem" in "Water Mask."

I appreciate the permission of CJ Muchhala to reprint her poem "Moths" in "Recalibration."

Two names were changed in the text to protect privacy.

Library of Congress Cataloging in Publication Data

Names: Devine, Monica, author.
Title: Water mask / by Monica Devine.
Description: Fairbanks, Alaska : University of Alaska Press, [2019] |
    Includes bibliographical references. |
Identifiers: LCCN 2018032190 (print) | LCCN 2018044293 (ebook) | ISBN
    9781602233737 (ebook) | ISBN 9781602233720 | ISBN 9781602233720 (paper :
    acid free paper)
Subjects: LCSH: Devine, Monica. | Intuition. | Speech
    Therapist—Alaska—Biography. | Self-realization.
Classification: LCC BF315.5 (ebook) | LCC BF315.5 .D48 2019 (print) | DDC
    818/.603dc23
LC record available at https://lccn.loc.gov/2018032190

for Asher

CONTENTS

This is not a story, only life.
Alice Munro

It is not down on any map; true places never are.
Herman Melville

MISSION OF MOTHERHOOD

I do not know much about gods,
but I think that the river is a strong brown god.
T. S. Eliot

I used to carry my baby like that. Just like the young woman did in the story Agnes told. I carried him in a pack on my back, an internal frame pack we used on camping trips to carry sleeping bags and gear. My husband fashioned it into a baby carrier by cutting holes in the nylon fabric where our little boy poked his chubby legs through.

Riding high up off the ground, my baby would hold onto the tubing at the top of the pack and push down with his feet at my hips. He babbled and jumped up and down when I caught a batch of fish in our dip-net. Carrying him was easy; I was young and lean, my arms and legs strong. He was never too heavy to shoulder, not like the 70 plus pounds of fish we hauled out of the canyon in army surplus packs.

This is how I first heard the story from Agnes at the Mendeltna Creek Lodge, a roadhouse where I often stop for lunch on my way to our cabin in Tazlina. Agnes, a stranger then, sat at the bar eating a bowl of soup. She was of a thin, wiry build, with long graying hair roped into a braid that hung clear to her waist. Her voice was thick and gravelly, like she had smoked away her years. She spoke of the two kids who recently drowned in the icy waters of Long Lake when their mother lost control of her car on the steep snow-blown mountain road.

"Deaths like that happen a lot out this way," she said. "There were those two little kids who were caught in a sweeping fire that burned down their cabin one winter, when it hit close to 30 below."

Agnes leaned to one side on the bar stool, stretching out her back. She tore off a piece of bread and chewed it slowly. Recalling children who had died over the years, she said, "The little ones are those you don't forget. They never had a chance, never got a proper hook on life." And she began another story about a young woman dip-netting on the Copper River with her baby on her back.

It's necessary, if you're going to place a net in the river, to watch the water and get familiar with its ways. Be aware of the current, the likely path the fish are taking, how much debris is in the water. Take note of the water level and the condition of the bank. You have to watch how the wind disturbs the surface so you know where to cleanly place your net down deep, way below the riffles.

The Athasbacan Indian women knew these things by heart. They fished the Copper River and the Tazlina, Tonsina, Gulkana, and Klutina Rivers ("na" means water *or* river*) for hundreds of years. They knew where the good fish runs were, how to skin and gut a salmon, how to prepare it for drying on racks in the sun, how to pre-serve the meat in their smokehouses. The women took their babies everywhere they went in all kinds of weather. While fishing, they securely strapped their babies in cradles made from the strong branches of birch trees.*

"It happened a long long time ago," Agnes said.

I sensed a sadness bloom around her, a deep hurt that floated somewhere behind her eyes. She continued.

The young couple was fishing the river for the first time, learning how to dip their nets by watching others in the canyon. The woman cared for her baby tenderly, pulling her arms through a warm sheepskin coat and covering her feet with wool socks. It can get cold in the can-yon, even when the sun is riding high in the sky. She bundled her baby into her backpack and stepped onto a huge rock that jutted into the fast water. She reached over the rocks and eased her long pole, with its large round net, into the current.

Soothed by the smell and the rhythm of the river, she held her net steady and waited.

It wasn't long before she felt a bump in the net. Hand over hand she pulled the pole toward her, feeling her arms burn with each pull. Her baby clapped her hands and made happy babble sounds, craning her neck to watch her mom pull in the fish. Before taking the fish out of the net, the woman bonked them over the head with her fish whopper to settle them down a bit. They flopped around her feet, straining against the net, their gills pumping in the cool dry air. With a few swift cuts she sliced the gills, flipped the fish over, and bled them out. Then she slid the pole back into the water and waited. Her husband stood a little ways downriver, she and the baby always in his peripheral vision as he too worked his pole, dipping for fish.

Sometimes things happen with such swiftness you wonder if they really happened at all. There's a hazy line between one instance of reality and another—where one begins and ends is lost to you.

She was screaming though her husband couldn't hear her cries above the roar of the river; he could just see her arms flung out in front of her, her hands reaching toward the muddy water. Then she fell to the ground and held onto the rocks as the shock, like lightning, coursed through her trembling body.

Her screaming turned into deep, heavy sobs and it was only then her husband realized what had happened. Her backpack was empty. When she bent over to pull her pole in on another sweep of the eddy, their baby slid head first out of the pack and splashed into the roaring hydraulics of the current, sucked down instantly by silt.

He scanned downriver and saw no trace of their baby girl, then scrambled over the rocks to reach his wife.

Agnes put on her glasses and took a look at her bill. We'd been yakking for close to an hour. We said our goodbyes and parted ways. On the rest of my drive I thought of how many times I had cheated death, in a way, or maybe put others in harm's way as unknowingly as the young woman in the story.

I used to carry my baby that way. In a pack on my back.

From O'Brien Creek Road we walked the old Copper River railroad grade, where a Fish and Game biologist once told us, *travel at your own risk*. The climb down to the river was rough, a steep bank with loose rocks, and there was always the possibility of encountering bears. Down we hiked to a rocky outcropping where the boiling river funneled between steep canyon walls. On the gravel bar my ankles grazed flowers growing riverside, dwarf fireweed and Siberian aster. A fresh breeze kept the bugs away.

To find a good eddy site I threw a stick in to see where the water was flowing, opposite the main current. In those eddies where the water is slow, the fish gather to rest, taking a break from their frantic swim upriver to their natal spawning grounds. My net stayed open with the rush of the current, and the fish swam in, easy as could be. Sometimes only one fish would come. Other times, on a good run, I could max out on my limit in half an hour.

Red salmon aren't fighters. We caught them not for sport but for food, eschewing shrink-wrapped, farm-raised, processed foods offered in the supermarket aisles. I dragged the long-handled net in and out of the water, scooping for salmon, with my one-year-old baby springing up and down on my back, giggling and clapping his hands in a game of patty-cake. I was joyful securing our own food, healthy food that was as much a part of our lives as breathing.

Memories flooded my mind as they often do on long drives, with nothing left to distract but mountains in the distance and river corridors that snake the winding road I was traveling.

A favorite hiking area, along the historic Iditarod Trail is a perfect place to ski when the snow is good. One wintry day, cold but not too cold, around 22 degrees, I bundled up my baby and headed for the trailhead. I've always enjoyed Nordic skiing, relying on my own power to track trails in the woods and along frozen riverbeds. On skis, when rocks and bumpy roots are blanketed with snow, I'm able to cover more miles and move much faster down the trail.

The air was crisp after a fresh snowfall and the snow, loose and powdery. I picked up my pace as the snow swooshed beneath my feet and congratulated myself on aspiring to a substantial workout, while giving my baby a healthy day outdoors in the cold and sun.

Though the day stretched out in front of me, I was well aware of the shifting conditions of light that time of year, when the sun leaves early, turning the day into twilight. My baby was fast asleep in my pack. Kick, glide. Kick, glide. How relaxing the physical ease my body felt in the cold, clean air. How soothing it was for my little boy, who sensed my smooth, effortless rhythm as he snuggled down into the pack for a nap. Two miles in, I thought: the time going in is equal to, or could be even greater than, the time going out, depending on many factors. An important point to remember no matter the time of year.

My baby was asleep and happy. I kept moving, just another mile. It was sunny and beautiful and so easy-going.

A half mile more and I felt my baby's lumpy body wiggle in the pack. He woke up with a distressing cry, sounds I'd never heard him make before. Raw screeching sounds like he was in great pain. I turned around and skied over my fresh tracks, bound for the safety of the trailhead. The movement and rhythm of my body that so often soothed him made no difference. His screaming cries escalated. What could be so wrong?

I stopped, lifted him from the pack, and pressed my hand to his skin. His hands and feet, chest and ears were cold. Because he was quiet, I'd assumed he was fine. I didn't think about body temperature and how it drops when you sleep. Not hearing any fussy complaints, I didn't think the cold was affecting him. He was dressed properly, covered head to toe in a wool hat, snowsuit, mittens, and down booties.

I unzipped my coat and held him against me while I hobbled down the trail, dragging my ski poles behind me. Pressing his body into mine, I carried him as I did in his infancy, cuddled on my chest. We'd skied that way many times when he was only a few months old. But now it made no difference.

His crying grew more desperate. I considered removing clothes and touching skin to skin to elevate his temperature, but that seemed risky. Instead I zipped him up inside my coat and hoped for the best. Warm tears rolled down my cheeks. I'd always been able to soothe the cries of my baby.

Back home a long soak in a warm bath brought him back to his old self, the happy babbling baby for whom my love was as high and wide as the sun-soaked sky. But I had been tested in that protective wing of motherhood, guilty for not paying close enough attention, for dropping the ball on his safety by the seduction of the day.

Another incident crossed my mind. The time he slipped into the water from the tube of a raft while we were lazily sunning on a lake. I was changing his diaper when he started kicking and giggling, and in a split second he slid off the tube right under my hands. He floated on his back with a look of total calm on his face. No harm done. He was within easy reach. Still.

I squirmed in my seat thinking of other incidents. Of so many times when we took our boys into the wild, trusting we'd be looked after if we just thought about the hazards ahead of time, paid close attention, dressed them for the weather. We didn't make far-reaching changes in our way of life when they were born into ours. We simply blended them into our everyday experiences because that is the way we lived.

If it is true that the education of a child begins in the womb and that a fetus learns through the actions of its mother, I hoped my children would not grow insular and be stymied by fear when they were older. Activities in the backcountry would prepare them for life, I thought. They would ski and climb mountains, hike trails, and raft rivers. Hopefully our lifestyle would teach them to adapt to life's changing conditions with confidence.

Some people say the woman who lost her baby to the river was not paying attention; that she brought death to her door through her own perilous ways. The young woman was so focused on her fishing, she completely forgot about her baby.

The fact that her child's tomb was sealed in the dull brown waters of the river would never change. For the rest of her life, the loss of her baby would stick in her mind like burnt milk in a pot. There is no greater punishment. And as sure and clean as the curve of a mountain, she would question *why* in a million different ways until the day she dies.

If I had just tied myself off with a short rope and anchored myself to a tree, maybe then I wouldn't have leaned so far over the rock, taking chances. Maybe we shouldn't have gone down into the canyon at all. Why didn't we just drive to the bridge and dip-net from the beach? We could have fished where the land is flat and where kids are running around skipping rocks in the river and roasting hotdogs and marshmallows over driftwood fires. We didn't need to fish the eddies. We could have caught just as many fish by sweeping the net in slow water, walking safely along the beach. Oh, God, why didn't we? Why?

I read of old Native lore that said if you remove dirt and snow from your porch by sweeping it every day, your baby will learn to live a good clean life. If you keep your baby from crying so hard she can't catch her breath and flails her arms like a bird, you are a good mother. And after you carefully clean a fish you should return its bones to the river so it can be restored and continue on its path to the place where it was first birthed. If you point the salmon's head upriver, its spirit is sure to find its way home.

Unlike the salmon, that poor baby's spirit would never find a home. She would wander the earth afraid and confused. Riding on the wind that rips through trees, she would cry for her mother, endlessly.

The Copper River, it is said, never gives up its dead. No matter what, the water always wins. Its murky current unmoors trees, wears down rock, and roars between steep canyon walls, scarring the land like it scarred so deeply that young woman's life.

My heart aches for the woman who lost her baby to the river though it happened so many years ago. Agnes never forgot about the little ones who died. As mothers we don't forget. Once on a mission of motherhood, we are always a mother, to our own and to all children everywhere.

I got the impression by the small flecks of sadness in her eyes, that perhaps Agnes wore the remembrance of all those children on her sleeve as a badge of honor. Maybe somewhere along the line she began to repeat their stories as penance to amend some unknowable actions taken when she herself lost a child. Maybe she, too, was another child's loving, imperfect mother.

I will never know.

INTERPRETING FROZEN GROUND

The only certain freedom is in departure.
Robert Frost

As poet Elizabeth Bishop once said, "When we travel anywhere, we are driving to the interior." I think she meant we follow the abiding voice within and walk the path to where that voice leads us. Moving to Alaska's Interior, a boundless stretch of mostly wilderness, wasn't solely a matter of geography, though the wilderness played a huge role in choosing where I would live. It was also a matter of simply trusting that initial voice of curiosity.

In 1978 with a freshly acquired master's degree in speech and language pathology, I applied for a job in three states: Montana, Wyoming, and Alaska. All of them generous with daunting sweeps of land and formidable windchill factors. I was looking for a place I could get lost in, a land of wide-open spaces that had the potential to ladle up a sense of adventure and possibility. Maybe even freedom from the repetitive nature of adult life I'd observed growing up.

Following my instincts, I left home and fell in love with *the freshness, the freedom, and the farness* of the north. Then stirred the question: What is this place all about and what kind of people live here?

I soon came to learn this was a place where anything was possible. A place where you could follow a dream and with hard work and a good dose of imagination realize that dream. Engaging experiences were part of the norm. Here was a place where women developed the skills to build their own houses and fly their own airplanes. These are roles I'd never seen played out by women in my secure suburban upbringing. Fresh from university on the heels of the women's rights movement, I knew more compelling ways of life were possible. Maybe even probable in the right place and time.

On one of my first work trips as an itinerant speech therapist, I traveled to a remote Alaska village along the Kuskokwim River. There I met a classroom teacher extraordinaire who earned the title "official resident baby catcher." But that wasn't all. A confident upbeat guy, he was also a bush pilot, a house builder, a businessman, a computer technician, a kid counselor, and if that wasn't enough, this father of five was a jack-of-all-trades who could fix your plumbing, grow his own food, and bake you a cake. Self-reliance born out of sheer need and necessity defined him and so many others I'd yet to meet.

You learn what you have to do by doing it, without an owner's manual. When forced to solve a problem or confront a life-or-death situation, you have to resist overthinking and steer clear of panic. The kind of stuff you don't learn in school, but in life.

One aviator friend tells the story of a guy he met at the local airport while he was busy tying down his own plane one chilly afternoon. A Super Cub flew over, banked, and landed, bouncing up and down as it rolled along the pitted runway. The thin wafer door flew open and out stepped a man wearing only shoes, socks, and underwear. Where in the world were his clothes?

At his previous destination, a gravel bar on the Koyukuk River, he inspected his plane before takeoff and took note of a flat tire. Super Cubs are infamous for their ability to take off and land in short distances. Their large balloon tires absorb impacts and can keep a plane afloat on uneven surfaces, like stretches of tundra and gravel bars.

Isolated with no immediate aircraft services or sources of compressed air, he did what any intelligent thinking person would do: he rolled up his pants, shirt, jacket, sleeping bag, a towel, rags—anything soft on hand—and stuffed them into the ailing tire. Forced to take a risky chance, through guts and pure genius, he took off and landed safely at his destination.

I was born and raised in Michigan. Winter is in my bones. But I never understood the meaning of true north until living at extreme northern latitude. Upon my arrival in Fairbanks, the temperature minus windchill was 33 degrees below zero. I stepped off the jet and into a frosted land of gently rolling hills accented by stands of puny black spruce trees. The buildings were covered in a bristly white icing, and the frigid air sparkled with diamond dust. Dry snow squeaked beneath my boots, and the hair in my nostrils froze.

That year's paralyzing cold snap lasted three consecutive weeks. I pushed back initial doubts during those dim-lit days and sought to interpret the frozen ground as best I could. There was something gripping and quixotic about confronting the task, however dark and cold the first impression.

There is a certain mystique to dry cabin living, "dry" meaning no indoor plumbing. The hills around Fairbanks are dotted with dry cabins, inhabited by all kinds of people who trade comfort for the experience of more thoughtful living. Or they are loners looking for a means of escape, or evangelists looking to "save" everyone in their orbit, or exiled outlaws looking to hide out in the wilderness. Some are looking to meet a challenge; others find the cheap rent agreeable to their budgets. We all had one thing in common—a shared propensity for going it alone, together.

Game nights under candlelight became a frequent pastime. Winter bonfires and potlucks drew us out of the dark corners of our cabins, except for the few loners in the bunch who craved no contact at all. Most of us assumed a tight huddle that was meant to keep everyone thriving and connected.

A mere five-mile commute from my cabin in the woods to my workplace in the city required thoughtful planning. I assembled a survival kit from the local army navy surplus store that offered every staple of cold weather gear: a goose-down-filled parka, sub-zero cold-weather gloves, bunny boots (good for up to -65 degrees Fahrenheit), a down-filled sleeping bag, and a collapsible snow shovel. I tossed the heap of goods into the trunk of my newly acquired used Honda Accord. If the car broke down, staying warm before help arrived was an imperative. Back then there were no backups to hang your lazy hat on, no data-driven cell phones to call for immediate roadside service. I imagined succumbing to hypothermia in a bone-chilling broken-down vehicle, its gas tank along with all my options, sucked dry. Best to be fully prepared.

I enjoyed the exercise of chopping wood and hauling water and working outside in all manner of weather. Heating water for cooking and washing dishes forced me to slow down and live more conscientiously, to pay attention to simple everyday activities for my survival. Though hard-wrought, the experience gave me confidence and satisfaction in my abilities to live alone. Not to mention a shot of memorable romanticism: On wintry nights I walked a narrow trail to the outhouse, a flashlight beam lighting my way. On those tomb-still nights when the drapery of a neon green aurora staggered across the sky, I'd snap off my flashlight and stand watching for as long as I could muster, wrapped in the pleasure of a golden silence I'd never known before.

Nearing March I craved color and wondered when the ground would green up. As the months passed, I likened my living to a mole's scurrying the confines of a long narrow tunnel. I was benumbed by the cold, its newness wearing off. Time to dig out and resurface. My visions of mud puddles and T-shirts were just around the corner. Or were they?

Would breakup happen all at once? How long till my daily dressing of long underwear, wool socks, and bunny boots be replaced with sleeveless summer dresses and sandals? Part of the charm of the Interior was that the long, cold winters would be followed by 20-hour-long sunlit days during the peak of summer. Eventually life would arouse from its deep winter sleep.

The snowpack melted quickly that first year. As the warming sun returned, the snow around my cabin shrank into tiny islands of slushy puddles. From that point forward change came swiftly. Cottonwood buds burst open into shimmering neon green. Birds and small animals dug themselves out and chimed in with their rustlings and noise. The air smelled sappy and sweet. The long-awaited turn of season could never arrive too soon and, in subsequent years, always felt like the very first time.

One wintry day months after my arrival in Fairbanks, I was eating dinner at the Hungry Dog, a small restaurant that served up vegetarian fare. I'd grown attached to the place, often skipping meal preparations at home. Some nights it took all my energy just to keep the woodstove stoked at the cabin and the five-gallon jugs of water from freezing. The routine was to shower as necessary at the University of Alaska field house and have dinner in town before driving back out to the cabin. On one occasion, a tall handsome man entered the restaurant, stomped his boots, shook snow off his hat, and looked my way.

"May I join you?" he asked politely. "My name's Kent."

I said yes.

He too was from the Midwest, Iowa, the only one to leave his immediate family, where grandparents helped raise babies and where brothers lived down a dusty road and just across the pasture. He had found work on a construction crew with the Trans-Alaska pipeline and labored under the snowcapped mountains of the Wrangell–St. Elias Range. The mountains captured his affections and a return to the rolling cornfields of Iowa shrank away like an image in a rearview mirror.

I soon began the leisurely move from my rustic cabin to his work-in-progress house, also plumbing and electricity-free. The 24-by-24-foot barn-style house stood on a hill in the middle of a five-acre parcel of birch and spruce stands in Fox, a small settlement north of Fairbanks. An inspiring view of the natural world was top priority in our house-building goals. We installed voluminous windows taking in the views of all directions except north, where the sun in winter didn't much shine anyways.

We installed 12 inches of insulation between the walls for nearly soundproofed living spaces. Just a short distance down the road, we fetched water from a gushing artisan well. We skied the rolling hills of Fox in subzero temperatures (nearly missing frostbite a time or two) and assembled an assortment of sled dog puppies eager to pull sleds and humans on our daylong excursions.

I had an encompassing desire for wanting more—not more stuff—but more challenging, life-enhancing experiences. We nurtured a homestead mentality, working hard to map out a life that followed our inward aesthetics. I ground grains into flour for bread and made healthy meals from scratch. My garden yielded an abundance of vegetables under the long, light-filled days of summer. We witched the ground for a good well site and after a year were hooked up to power. We measured and cut and nailed, completing the house's interior before the next mind-numbing winter dug in its heels.

I was happy to explore this engaging landscape, now with a partner who introduced me to many "first times." We kayaked local rivers and explored the forests outside our backdoor. The initial meeting of my husband was not, at least consciously, love at first sight. What sealed the proposal was an observation brought to light through memory of one of my mother's dictates: *Marry a man who is good with his hands.*

The meaning of her words took shape when we followed a change in jobs. We moved from the slow-paced country life of Fox to the bedroom community of Eagle River, just 15 miles from Anchorage.

It was summer, and we were hauling our belongings in a makeshift trailer, speeding along the 350-mile stretch of road from Fairbanks to Anchorage in our new pickup. There is only one direct route from Fairbanks to Anchorage. It's impossible to get lost. Our trusty GPS read only this: turn left and drive 350 miles south. That's it. There are no shortcuts. You drive the straight line and then you're there. All the way you're accompanied by wild rivers and forests and mountains. There are no yawning billboards or enticing gambling casinos. There are no alluring outlet malls, no fast-food open-all-night restaurants. A few small towns with churches and liquor stores and a smattering of lodges—the closest thing to home-cooked meals—are your main mileposts.

Glancing in the rearview mirror, Kent spied a problem. The plywood that formed a corner of the trailer had split apart. Our household belongings would soon litter the road if we didn't stop and make the necessary repairs.

He pulled out a box of tools from behind the driver's seat. Nailing the plywood back together wouldn't work; the continuous vibration would simply pry it apart again. The solution would require more innovative thinking.

Sitting in the truck cab, nose in a magazine, I heard banging and stepped outside to investigate. Kent was hammering rusty metal brackets onto the ends of the plywood, forming a sturdy corner.

"How in the world did you do that?" I asked.

"Simple. I just pounded the metal down flat and formed it around these pesky corners," he said.

"Where'd you get the metal?"

"I scrounged around the side of the road and found a couple old tin cans. This should do us for 100 or 200 more miles," he said.

It occurred to me then that creative problem-solving isn't a subject learned in academia. Huh. This would not be the first time I'd applaud his resourceful ways. There was another way of living, unbeknownst to me, where practical and inventive intelligence shined.

Surprisingly the move from Fox a couple years into our courtship was an easy decision, even in light of our newly built house. Moving south would bring more days of summer and significantly milder temperatures in the winter. Moving south would open a plethora of summer recreational options close by, like shrimping and fishing the waters of Prince William Sound. Our desire to explore new ground took hold like a shirttail on barbed wire—we were hooked.

Far from the meager hills of Fairbanks, we climbed the steep mountains that surrounded our new home in Eagle River. We skied the backcountry bowls without so much as a shiver. Gone was the shadow of ice fog and the ever-present alarm of frostbite nipping at our fingers and toes.

People move away from their birth homes for good reason. But I wondered about the desire for a certain landscape. Could geography win out over blood? Could the beauty of a vista be a stronger lure than the bonds of family in the decision to move away?

My first memories as a child were of our middle-class subdivision: the green manicured lawns and tree-lined streets busy with cars and kids on bikes. In the summer, kids' playful voices rose above the heat and humidity and always, always in the background was the constant low hum of road noise from the nearby interstate highway.

On the first snow of the season, we'd run outside in the thick of its gentle falling and stick out our tongues to receive whisper-light wafers of communion. The snow-globe world was quiet, safe, and holy. When the snow melted and water gushed along curbs and into sewer drains, we made boats out of sticks and sent them afloat in the runoff.

I was attentive to the world around me. Over time, new subdivisions duplicated like cells dividing, bringing more traffic and people. Shopping malls began to box us in and dominate the space around our rows of tiny houses. Dirt bike paths disappeared, hemmed in by fences. Shortcuts to the school playground were blocked off, forcing us to walk the long way around in busy traffic. Too much concrete, and not enough quiet, crept in while we weren't looking.

In spite of exploding growth I experienced golden moments, signal moments you could call them, when all the wild things—frogs and robins, rabbit holes, bats, and new grass—were intact in our small backyard. There the fleeting nature and fragility of life could still be touched and felt. I went to sleep at night thinking there would always be trees and hills and plants. There would always be snow and rain and stones, and somehow, they would stitch themselves together and make the world whole, as complete as it could ever be.

The village of Point Hope, Alaska, is the oldest continually occupied area in all of North America, an ancient place the Inupiat Eskimo have called home for over 10,000 years. *We don't come from someplace else,* they say. *We originated from the dirt. Our home is a place that has always been.*

On a work visit to the tiny whaling village, I walk a gravel spit lined with small houses set on pilings. Four-wheelers are parked out front and heating oil drums leveraged on wooden sawhorses hug the plywood homes. Satellite dishes flower here and there, bringing images of the modern world into the old. Beyond the village and opposite the sea line, a wide expanse of ochre tundra fans out until it meets the pristine blue horizon.

If you were to dig below the tundra scrub in Point Hope, it is likely you would excavate artifacts like thousand-year-old sled runners made of whale bone, implements carved from walrus ivory, and sharp-edged stone hunting tools. *We existed in the rivers and tundra, the mountains and deltas, as spirits before our birth.*

Where are one's roots and how deep do they grow? My own roots aren't nearly as ancient. I wasn't so attached to my Michigan roots to move back home in adulthood, and I'm curious about a people who stay in one place for longer than a few generations. My people do not think of themselves as originating from the womb of the earth. They come from countries in eastern Europe where boundaries and place-names were often in flux due to regional disputes and war.

But in Point Hope I am standing on top of prehistory where ancient relics are buried, layer upon layer of found objects that date back thousands of years. My eastern European origins put me back a couple hundred at best. Items passed down to me, the relics of my existence, include my grandmother's thin, gold wedding band from Austria, decorative buttons from my grandmother's sewing basket (buttons I took great pleasure sifting my fingers through as a child), and a set of Radford tableware crafted in the early 1950s. Though all our tools and crafts cast a look of fatigue and wear; in comparison, they were shiny and brand-new.

Unlike many Alaska Natives who have inhabited the same village for thousands of years, the history of my birth spans a scant few generations. I'd like to say I've come from the womb of the earth. I'd like to say I existed in the rivers and tundra, the mountains and deltas as a spirit before my birth. In the long view of human and geologic time and in an abstract reflective way, perhaps I have. But my people, like many inexperienced newcomers to Alaska, come from somewhere else. We staked our bearings and threw down stubborn roots until the ground decided to keep us here for good.

Today we live on a shelf above the Eagle River in the Chugach Mountain range. A dozen or so miles upriver lies Eagle Glacier, whose meltwater forms the brown silt river we kayak down on warm summer days. During the winter months, the river is a glassy ice highway you can skate away on when the conditions are just right.

I have lived here longer than anywhere else in my life. Do I lay claim to a place after 20 years, 40 or 50 years? I stand on this ground and am annihilated by its wild beauty. Another fierce winter wind will scald my cheeks. Another bending summer sun will invite activity well past a reasonable bedtime. I don't know how long it takes to claim a land as your own, but I do know what brought me here in the first place: curiosity and challenge and a deeply absorbing way of interacting with a wild land and its diverse people.

Maybe there is no need to possess this land or claim it as my own. It is enough to have fallen prey to its spell. Through its own dramatic pull, it has claimed me.

MANY THINGS WERE VISIBLE WHEN THE EARTH WAS THIN

Just now
A rock took fright
When it saw me,
It escaped
By playing dead.
Norbert Mayer

On a retreat in New Mexico, I woke up one morning and looked out at red clay mesas and sandstone chimneys propped up like cutouts against a coal-smudged sky. Only 50 feet from my door, the ground pushed up in mounds of red clay that begged my hands to sculpt pots. Rain spilled hard during the night (praise the sound of moody tin roofs), and I was surprised to see snow powdering the hills. Not unheard of in early October at 5,200 feet.

Only it wasn't snow. It was gypsum rock, an abundant mineral in the area that is usually covered with a thin layer of red dust that gets washed off by rain, then covered over again by wind. Up close the stones looked like Chiclets scattered over wide swaths of red clay.

I had climbed these hills many times, stepping on the tiny white stones knowing exactly what they were. But that's not how I saw them that morning. I raced into the ranch's kitchen to tell friends of my snowy discovery. As soon as the words left my mouth, I was reeling them back in with apology.

I thought of Anaïs Nin's famous quote: "We don't see things as they are; we see things as *we* are." One only sees what one knows. This is the time of year the mountain slopes of my Alaska home collect termination dust, signaling the transition from fall to winter. A change in light and a good washing after a night of hard rain made those tiny stones tumble into the foreground of my vision. Fresh from sleep I interpreted them as the first official snow of winter.

The experience of "different" seeing happens to me all too infrequently. I wish I could recreate a sudden jolt of perception through will or effort, but I can't. What I *can* do is stay alert and open to possibility so its occurrence won't pass me by unnoticed.

And then it happened again, though this time it was a sudden perception I couldn't make sense of. A summer day, late August. Driving home from a painting class, I was stunned by cotton-wood trees shaking with a vividness of color I'd never noticed before. A strong wind blew as the leaves twirled and vibrated in rhythmic waves. Varying shades of green pulsed through the leaves like light from a stroboscopic lamp.

I was not surprised to learn the word *strobos* means "an act of whirling," because that is precisely what happened. The leaves whirled against a backdrop of high-octane light. Had my right brain, the nondominant language side, taken over my perception temporarily? Was this a vision or an act of clear seeing? Or was it an altering of consciousness that bypassed thinking and went straight for the jugular: pure, ineffable awe?

To be fair, the vision, or whatever it was, lasted only a few seconds. But it felt like much more than simply witnessing pretty trees on the side of the road. What had caused such a jarring shift in perception, a sporadic moment of magic? Whatever it was I wanted more. I was having dinner with seasoned painters later that night. I could quiz them about the act of perception.

I wondered how artists are trained to see. Do they paint a mirror image of a scene or go for their own best interpretation? Perception is as unique as memory. A dozen people viewing the same scene paint it with wildly different perspectives.

One painter friend said he looks at the landscape and sorts elements related to shape. What is striking in the foreground? Where do strong lines meander, and do they move diagonally: left to right, up and down? What shapes stand out? Another friend said she keys into color and mood first and notices where light and shadows meet. Whether you are painting a landscape, an object, or a portrait, the interplay of light is central to how you will create the form.

Weeks later, walking a horse trail south of my casita, I saw a large misshapen stick on the side of the trail. I'm always careful to notice what is directly beneath my feet in the high desert, whether it be friend or foe. I toed the stick with the tip of my boot to view its other sides. The bottom was pocked and whitewashed. Clearly it was a bone, a single bone, probably from cattle. I walked on, prodding with my hiking pole, aware that I could run into a rattler. I spotted another stick, long and curvy, that looked like a snake, or was it just a twisted juniper branch that resembled a snake? I stepped back just in case. My eyes were playing tricks on me again.

Storm clouds idled above my head, a common late afternoon occurrence in these parts, and I walked faster to make it to shelter before the daily deluge. My stride kicked up dust, and I caught a glimpse of something dark, the size of a small backpack. It zipped past me in a blur and ducked under a spray of creosote bush. A jackrabbit perhaps. Quick movements and layers of shadow were tricking my sight as the darkening sky bled away color and definition.

You have to lose your mind before coming to your senses, a famous psychoanalyst once said. You have to lose the stickiness of thoughts, discard the roaming bandits of conceptualization, and let feeling and awareness have a say.

You have to know where you are in every moment, as horses do. Always alert, they prick their ears to unfamiliar sounds. They throw their heads back, inhale, and open their nostrils wide to new smells. Their sensate bodies are acutely aware as they draw information about everything around them.

Surely artists and photographers are privy to technical knowledge when they create, but intuition and feeling are equally as valuable. Led by their senses, artists become completely immersed in their subject matter. The late painter Georgia O'Keeffe sketched and painted thousands of landscapes of the acreage around her home in New Mexico. She walked the land daily, gathering the smell of the air, the mood of the sky, the color of the mesas when diffused by the light. She collected the weathered skulls and pelvises of deer and antelope for her studies, keying into the perception of starkness in the desert, and used a minimalist color palette to depict animal bones in her paintings.

In her pelvis series, using only blue and white paint, the bleached white bones look as though they are floating in space. A cerulean sky shows through the holes in the bones and gives the anatomy an abstract look. The forms appear ambiguous in shape and the contrasting effect of bleached white on the deepest of blue is stunning to the eye.

Sometimes I wonder if we humans aren't missing out on something. We know that because of the structure of their eyes, deer see color differently than we do. They see a bluer blue than we are able to perceive. Just as we humans can't hear some sounds, our eyes can't take in some elements of light, like the invisible wavelengths of ultraviolet and infrared. Deer sense colors toward the violet end of the spectrum so they can see a wider range of blues.

Would a deer see the blue of my jeans in a bluer blue than I see? Is there an enhanced world out there we're simply unable to process? Surely an artist's paintings would be more vivid and alive if her perception of the world was amplified. If we could perceive an enhanced range of color and light, everything around us would throb in an ultra-shimmering way, like my experience of the stroboscopic leaves. If our feelers were super sensitive though, it would be hard to manage such wild stimulation. We'd become unhinged.

"Many things were visible when the earth was thin," said Alma Keyes, a Yup'ik elder from Kotlik, Alaska. Keyes was speaking about the thin veil as she understood it through her ancient tribal people's worldview.

"Things were distinct when the land was thin," she said. "Not the way it is today."

Celtic mythology points to the notion of "thin places" too, where the visible and invisible worlds join, and we experience these thin places when we unexpectedly encounter shifts in perception or heightened states of mystery and joy, perhaps even in suffering.

My interpretation of the thin places, as experienced by ancient peoples, goes something like this: Imagine for a moment a hunter going after his prey as if his whole life depended upon it. There are no thoughts in his head other than the moment. He is not thinking about building a fire or what a clan member said earlier in the day. His attention does not stray from his immediate experience.

The hunter learns of the animal's thinking by examining its tracks: how the animal hesitates and turns, how it stops or stutters in its movements. Following his senses, he is ultra-aware of everything arising around him because his very existence depends upon it.

To call the animal out, the hunter may mimic its sounds. To experience the animal up close, he may make the same movements. Like a bird in suspended flight the hunter waits for the right moment to spring. He is focused and aware of his own actions and at the same time alert to the actions of the animal, the feel of the air, sounds of footfalls, sticks breaking under his feet, motion in the leaves. He imbibes a diffuse attention that includes everything around him, all at once. He is so attached to the animal's movements and rhythms that he and the animal become one. By worshipping the animal he is pursuing, the hunter adopts the material world as his spiritual world. He can turn into the animal he is seeking, and the animal becomes his guide in the spiritual realm.

Lest you think I'm a person, as you go, glance back at me! says the hunter to the animal. The hunter does not look up to the heavens and plead for a favorable outcome. This is unnecessary. The divine has its presence in every moment of his existence. In his world, everything is awake and aware: rocks, lakes, animals, wind—all things are brimming with consciousness. This may be why some people feel, wherever they go, they are among the spirits of their ancestors. Everything they encounter in life is considered with a bare reverence, a reverence that makes "the center hold." The direct immediacy of nature is what guides them through life events, their experiences requiring no filtering through a priest, rabbi, or guru for interpretation.

The psychological state of all of us is ruled by our patterns of attention. The veil between the object world and the self is clearly thin in young children, who are fully alive and engrossed in each experience and immersed in the pleasure of their senses without having any reflective thoughts about them. They simply enjoy a solid communion with each new and interesting moment. They don't stop and reflect. They don't make judgments. There is a clean slate between their perceptions and the object itself.

In piercing the veil, could I, too, become attuned to that which is invisible? I often find myself standing outside this circle of reciprocity with the moment, yearning to get in. I want to become part of the whole. If I could, at every turn, open to an expanded sense of seeing and feeling, then perhaps everyday moments in my ordinary life could be perceived with more depth and joy, even surprise.

Everything that exists can teach me something, I reason, if only I slow down and take notice. I can temporarily experience a thin veil like children do if I pay attention to something without desperation, longing, and judgment. Without having any kind of mental construct about the object or experience. If I drop my thoughts of past and future, my awareness will become razor sharp. If I converse with all the elements in my world, perhaps I would see that everything in my midst does indeed shimmer.

Marcel Proust said the secret of life is to be found in the art of attention, what he called "exaggerated attention." His writings describe pointed sensations of an activity where the mind is focused on minute details rather than thoughts of other things. Shifting our perception can lead us to other facets of reality.

When an old woman asked Buddha, how does one meditate, he replied: "Watch your hand when you draw water from the well." That is all. He succinctly described meditation in motion, a way to become immersed in the task at hand, a way to relax the mind of unnecessary thinking, like the ancient hunter does.

Proust wrote that shining awareness on the task at hand may lift the ennui people often feel, the sense of dread as if their lives are passing them by. If we mindfully observe the small things as Proust did in his famous description of becoming completely immersed in savoring a madeleine steeped in tea, our absorption in the moment will set us free. With vivid awareness of the tastes and smells of the experience, there would be no dread in the moment. And if we could keep it up, there would be no dread in the next moment, or the one after that, and the one after that.

Now I finally understood the meaning of the words from the poet William Blake: "If the doors to perception were cleansed, everything would appear to man as it is . . . infinite."

Another way we can pierce the veil and feel totally alive is when we are in the presence of great beauty. We can be delivered naturally to a heightened state of awareness when we take part in great art, music, and poetry. In these moments, our mind is idle, and time and space cannot touch us.

On a recent trip to Italy, I was rapt by the beauty of the exquisitely carved, replicated statue of *David*. I slowly circled the work of art, gripped with awe by its beauty. The statue was so engrossing, for long moments I simply couldn't look away. In those moments, *the I that is me disappeared*. A seamless place rarely noticed in my everyday life took over and my thinking mind stopped.

I once read of a rare psychological disorder in which foreign tourists standing in the presence of miraculous beauty were rushed to the psychiatric ward of Florence's Santa Maria Nuova Hospital. One woman collapsed while viewing a Raphael painting. Another panicked at the foot of Bernini's *Ecstasy of Saint Teresa*. I don't know if this is true.

Immersed in the serenity and power of *David*, I was glad to have left there sans an episode of fainting. Though breathless, I think I may have come close.

Shifts of perception can be remarkable in the natural world too, even in modern times. Wild animals often cross our paths by way of scent and movement and sometimes just by plain curiosity of the human-hiker-woman wandering the tundra, passing through their mountain homes. Never before had I experienced so deep a connection with a wild animal as the face-to-face meeting with a hoary marmot I surprised on a rocky outcropping while hiking up to a chain of alpine lakes. To be honest, he wasn't the least bit surprised; I was the one who stopped, stunned in her tracks.

After climbing a steep slope flanked by hemlock, I paused to rest where the tree line turned to alpine tundra. Blue, glacier-scarred ponds decorated the terrain. Rounding a bend, farther up the trail, I was startled to see a huge marmot sunning on a flat rock about 10 feet above me. He sat calmly on the bedrock bench, observing his world like a king surveying his kingdom. He was resting, perhaps, after his daily occupation of digging burrows and searching for food. Taking in the afternoon sun, he lounged unperturbed by my presence.

Silently I stepped off the trail and when I stopped, he noticed my movement. He looked sidelong into my eyes. Now we were taking a great interest in each other. Alert for predators, marmots sometimes make loud whistles when alarmed, but he remained quiet and still. Our gaze held.

I could feel my physicality, the material sense of my body in relation to his. I was watching him, and he was watching me. I wondered how long our encounter would last. His gray coat rippled in the wind. Neither of us flinched. In a momentary trance, our sentience melded.

David Abrams, in *Becoming Animal,* writes, "Many undomesticated animals move in a fairly constant dialogue, not with themselves but with their surroundings. It is not an isolate mind but rather the sensate, muscled body itself that is doing the thinking.

It is a kind of distributed sentience, this intelligence in the limbs and body."

The marmot sat motionless, sniffing the air, the smooth arc of his body still. He continued watching me until I finally broke gaze.

I was not drawn to this charming moment by the tundra grasses stirring around me or by the magnificent blue alpine ponds; those were beautiful sights to consider, all alive in my peripheral vision. I was drawn to the moment by an act of absorption as this motionless animal split my perception like a boat's bow through water.

In a sudden shift in awareness, I became fused in an event of spontaneous interaction where my gaze lingered in the eyes of a wild animal. I imagined him thinking: What is this long-legged creature carrying a heavy backpack and sporting a bouncy ponytail? I stepped back onto the trail feeling refreshed and alive.

Tin skies. A cold fall day. I am walking a beach on the shores of the Bering Sea in Nome, Alaska. Waves break the shoreline as a cold wind bruises my cheekbones. I zip my hood and cinch its ruff around my face. Sifting through stones, I notice a white one with a pale blue vein running through its middle. I bend over and pluck it from the gripping sand and stroke it between my fingers. Its presence in my hand seems to light up as the graying sea and sky shrink into the periphery. An ordinary stone to be sure but as I hold it in my hand, I give it vitality.

I claim the stone as mine. I rub it between my fingers, feeling its cool contours and admiring its subtle beauty. I remember reading about a shamanic practice called "rock seeing," in which you choose a rock that gathers your attention, hold it in your hand, and simply observe. Besides noting its physical features, I ask myself what type of wildness resides within this stone? Where has it been? Where is it going?

Cold to the touch, I think, there are stories in this stone. Awash and carried by stormy seas, it has been pushed, tumbled, and coughed up on this shore. It has seen many things over the ages. Perhaps stacked in a heap on the beach, where someone built a small cairn, marking a trail for others to find their way. Or maybe part of an ancient or contemporary ritual, where each member of a tribe or family whispers a prayer to the stone and then stacks them on the grave of their beloved.

I believe we have the perceptual ability to *extend* our awareness out into the world, and not solely with living things. Baudelaire observed, "Man walks through forests of physical things that are also spiritual things, that watch him with affectionate looks." The rock will respond once I make the decision to become an active member in the reciprocity of its nature. All I have to do is feed the rock with my thoughts and consider it an object of reflection. In turn, it prizes me with an image or feeling that heightens my curiousity.

I put the stone in my pocket and carry it home with me, aligning it on a shelf in my studio. We would talk again later.

On a cold early morning at my casita in New Mexico, I hear a slight wind gearing up outside. The sound is eerie at first, a low nasal humming. Picking up momentum, it makes an instrument of my vibrating clothesline; my jeans and towels rise up, slap-flapping. Updrafts gather under the outdoor chairs, shaking all sorts of metal parts. Even the windowpanes are shaking in their casings.

I open the screen door and step out. I'm a large woman, and I can hardly stand up in the turmoil. I look across the yard to where the wind, blowing in all directions, bangs against a lonely horse trough, causing a ruckus wherever it touches,

And then, just when I think its momentum is nearing a peak, it stalls. Quells in an instant. Where did it go? Just as suddenly it drums up again, the wail strengthening in layers. A dust devil coils, then lets loose. I watch and wait for the fury to die out, licking my lips of grit.

Apparently I can't trust my seeing *or* my hearing. I'm not always 100 percent sure of my perceptions and what the wild elements are trying to tell me. Intuitively I know the afternoon heat that bears down as I climb mesas in the high desert is remembered in my body in the same way as when I'm walking a cold sand beach on the Bering Sea. Both places possess their own particular mysteries, remembered when my senses and my heart remain open.

I praise the mountain energy night and day, said the female mystic poet Mirabai. *I walk the path that ecstatic human beings have taken for centuries.*

ON THE EDGE OF ICE

Utqiagvik, 1997

Why are we so susceptible to the charm of these landscapes when they are so empty and terrifying?
Jean-Baptiste Charcot

As far north as one can travel in Alaska, a good 300 miles above the Arctic Circle, a string of small coastal villages speckle the landscape on a vast backdrop of snow and sea and ice. The villages span an area of 500 miles, east to west, and starve for light in the winter months. By late November the sun makes its final exit, dipping below the tundra line, not showing its face again until the end of January.

Of all my travels, these small villages at the top of the world—locked in a snowy darkness in winter and void of vegetation but for thick tundra grasses in the shortened summers—intrigue me most. Only there have I seen a cerulean sky vibrant against thick May snows, a color I could not reproduce on film though I have tried many times, a color that makes my heart leap. The seeming emptiness of the Arctic is magical. Especially the sea ice.

I would soon learn of the unfathomable power of sea ice and how, once it starts moving, absolutely nothing can stop it.

One early December visit, as our plane descended over Utqiagvik (formerly known as Barrow), I scanned the sky and land looking for a distinction between the two. There was nothing to view but a void of dull gray space. The plane shuddered and hummed as we circled for 20 minutes, waiting for an opening. Just before touchdown, I wondered about the status of our fuel tank.

Finally the grid of town became visible and an array of street-lights stabbed the early morning fog. On the other side of this manufactured light, the frozen tundra extended into a vast and dark emptiness that at a glance, belied feasible life.

On the ground, ice fog shrouded buildings and exhaust coughed from trucks, buses, and cars. Utqiagvik, population around 4,600, is the largest and northernmost settlement on the shores of the Beaufort Sea. It offers a modern grocery store, a generous public library, and an Inupiat Cultural Center that vividly interprets the people's lifestyle past to present, highlighting the juxtaposition of land and people in one of the harshest places on earth.

The following day I set out early morning and walked a gravel road that parallels the shoreline. Though the skies were clear, it was still dusky, and the bright snow offered but a paltry light. The temperature hung at 10 below, worsened by a heavy-handed wind scouring the streets of town. The sea was black and choppy, and water lapped the beach in curls of flimsy white foam.

After work I walked the beach back to my hotel room and was surprised to see house-sized chunks of ice chaotically littering the shoreline. The enormous blocks had migrated shoreward from the North Pole ice pack and were stacked on top of each other at all kinds of wonky angles. Weirdly stark and naked, they looked like they'd been dropped from outer space.

By nightfall the wind and tide pushed the runaway blocks back out to sea. Remarkably in a brushstroke of time the blocks disappeared, the wind died, and the sea became eerily flat as though nothing monumental had occurred there at all.

I had never before thought of ice as being old or young, new or rotting. But after spending weeks in the Arctic throughout various seasons, I have come to understand how ice never knows stillness. While traveling near the coastal village of Point Hope in a small plane, I made a mental note of the directions printed on the door: "To open, hold button in, pull handle." I rehearsed this in case we went down: how to open the door if it were not wedged into sea ice; if water did not wash over us in the heap of freezing twisted metal. In a world parallel to ours the unimaginable happens. Only weeks before, a similar plane crashed when immense fog closed in just before touchdown. Five whalers—brothers, sons, and fathers—were tragically pulled through the slipknot of eternity in a plane that nose-dived into young sea ice.

Over the past few decades, warmer temperatures have permeated the villages on the Arctic coast. It was once common, by the end of September, for large masses of ice to break off the northern ice pack and migrate south, connecting with the ice on shore. The shorefast ice was reliable and solid enough for travel. Now villagers note how the ice is breaking up earlier in spring and freezing later in winter, sometimes as late as January.

Thin ice makes it difficult to travel by snow machine to traditional whaling hunting grounds many miles off shore. Warm temperatures, too, are cutting into people's recreational activities. "We used to go riding around on the sea, just for fun, until the beginning of June," one elder told me. "But this year the ice is too thin."

A sign that reads Whale Spoken Here hangs in the arctic entryway of Daniel Akootchook's small wood-framed home in Kaktovik, a village on Barter Island east of Utqiagvik. A picture of the Last Supper hangs above his kitchen table next to a British Petroleum Exploration calendar and a sprawling geological map of the Arctic National Wildlife Refuge. Whale muktuk and blubber for the dogs fill a huge metal bowl next to the door. A six-foot strip of baleen from a bowhead whale graces the far wall. As a retired whaling captain, Daniel feeds my fascination with the perennial behavior of sea ice through his personal recollections. Daniel is a funny guy and colors his stories with flourishing gestures; his body seems to dance to an old Eskimo song as he talks.

"Sometimes we go 10, 20 miles out," he says. "Way, way out. We never know when whale will come. If it gets too windy, ice could break up so we wait. Wait for good weather. If it's too windy, we don't take chances on whaling. For our safety, and for whale's safety, too."

Daniel shows me an old iron whaling gun with no scope that is used to shoot the whale after it has been harpooned, should this measure be necessary. "The heart is targeted, halfway between flipper and eye. A small bomb inside harpoon explodes and kills whale. Most good whalers use just harpoon, with a sharp tip and a float. Today we use floats white man makes. Before, we used seals. My mother used to take meat out, take blubber out through the seal's mouth. Clean it, dry it out, and attach it to a rope. It floats. Works pretty good." Daniel recalls memories of the centuries-old ritual with a sparkle in his eyes.

The whalers speak best to changing weather patterns over the years. What used to be a 20-mile snow machine ride across solid pack ice is now only 3 miles through unpredictable pressure ridges. Summers are becoming warmer and springs stormier. As the summer ice melts, seawater absorbs the sun's energy and warms the ocean even further.

Daniel spoke of the need for refrigeration in the storage of whale meat as cellars dug into the permafrost to store marine mammals are now beginning to thaw. For the first time in its history, the residents of Utqiagvik recently experienced a thunderstorm, witnessing thunder and lightning that is rarely, if ever, seen along the Arctic coast.

Apart from the human toll, warming trends of the Arctic sea ice has created less habitat for many marine mammals. Ringed and bearded seals require an ice-bound ecosystem for pupping and finding food. Walrus need ice thick enough to hold their weight and thin enough to break through to breathe. And polar bears are finding it harder to hitch a ride on platforms of moving ice from which they hunt seals.

Instead they are showing up closer to town. Residents have every reason to worry when the bears come too close, sniffing for an easy meal. Imagine sending your kids to school in the morning, only to find huge polar bear tracks between the school bus and your own front door.

One spring on a visit to Utqiagvik, I was invited to travel out on the ice with a young Inupiat man to watch a whaling crew keep vigil. The crew hunted bowhead whale, also called "ice whale" because they travel under the ice. Bowheads can be up to 60 feet long, and weigh close to 75 tons.

Adhering to tradition, my guide was required to ask the whaling captain for permission to bring along an outsider. One whaler looked me over and inquired if I was with child; due to the inherent dangers, pregnant women are not allowed out on the ice. I had a camera with a long lens that I kept zipped up in my parka, snug and free from the frigid May air. Satisfied, the whaler nodded. I was good to go.

My guide, John, carried a rifle on his back to ward off polar bears, and he wore a white traditional whaling parka to blend in with the austere landscape. The trail was coarse and bumpy. Bouncing along, we skirted massive chunks of sea-foam ice sculpted in the midday sun. We stopped to view polar bear tracks filled with frost crystals, probably a day old, and over twice as big as John's footprint.

After a whale or seal catch, polar bears often follow snow machine tracks if scented with blood or seal oil. We didn't have a catch of any kind on board, yet for the remainder of the ride I kept a steady surveillance over my shoulder.

Miles away from the comforts of town, the ice was equally dangerous and breathtaking. The sea horizon or—one could call it the ice horizon—unfolded in all directions, dreamlike against a white-washed sky. The air felt pure and refreshing, as smooth and real as a glass of cold white wine.

We traveled another couple of miles over small rippled waves until the trail narrowed into even, hard-packed snow. Negotiating wiry switchbacks, John swerved us around piles of crushed sea ice. Arriving at camp, we parked the snow machine and walked to the ice edge. Two other whaling crews were set up in white tents along a wide linear crack in the ice known as the lead (pronounced leed). Each captain flew a distinctive flag, emblazoned with his initials and markings that held personal meaning or humor. An ancient symbol adorned one flag; a simple happy face adorned another. The colorful flags hung motionless in the frigid air.

The deep black sea eclipsed the crusted ice edge. Earlier John had told me to take note of the horizon as we traveled the sea ice; to look where the pressure ridges and ice fan out to meet the skyline. You can tell there's an open lead by looking at the color of the line. It's dark and gray where there is open water; it's white and light blue, where there is not.

Now I looked down at my boots, hovering on the edge of ice, and watched points of light shimmer on the water. The gradation between ice and water was distinct, like standing on the edge of two separate worlds, each boundless and titanic. Bloodstained snow under my boots was evidence of a whale taken a week prior. Nearby a young boy sat atop a hummock, the crushed sea ice piled 15 feet beneath him, and patiently scanned the horizon. The air was silent, the men still, watching and waiting for a whale to call their name.

A small whale, a beluga, surfaced 20 feet in front of us, its smooth white body lifting and plunging in an unbroken rhythm. Next came a seamless pod of choreographed movement, dozens of belugas swimming like porpoises close enough to touch from the ice edge. The whalers watched and waited, desiring the bowhead—the only baleen whale with a range restricted to icebound seas—for their catch.

John said the bowhead is our brother. He told me it is the whale that ultimately decides when it will come and offer itself to the crew. The process can never be hurried. The whale is shot with a hand-held harpoon with a darting gun attached. From an umiaq, a skiff-like boat made from sealskin that is quiet in the water, the whalers navigate the rough and icy waters and must get very close to the whale to obtain a clear shot. John told me the whale is then floated back to the ice for butchering. He spoke of catching the multiple-ton mammal in an elegant way, with sharp attention to detail.

The whalers practiced enduring patience. Some remained unmoving in umiaqs, or aluminum skiffs, ready to shove into the sea when the time was right. Others watched from the ice edge with their weathered hands clasped around mugs of hot tea, making mental notes of subtle shifts in clouds and wind and temperature.

The bowhead whale's eyesight is poor; perhaps it's adapted to living its days under dark, murky water. But it hears well—the sounds of men on ice, their heavy footfalls walking to and from the tents. Under the faint light of evening that never entirely turns dark, the sun's reflection dissipated and a light mist hovered over the open lead. A gentle wind blew a veil of weightless snow over our feet. We had spent hours waiting and watching. For reasons unknown to us, today the bowhead decided not to arrive.

We readied to leave. In a quiet voice, John told me if south-southwest winds pick up, the crew would be disappointed. The winds could completely close the lead. He motioned us past the tents to the row of shiny red and yellow snow machines, their arresting blots of color a peculiar mixture of modern technology and a hunting ritual as ancient as man himself. Hundreds of ducks in a spattered V clamored overhead. Moments later a hundred more skimmed the water's surface and then flushed upward in a rush of activity. We turned our backs to the sea and began the rugged ride back to solid ground.

I heard remarkable stories from the elders, of their lives on the ice prior to the 1960s and the advent of snow machines. In one, a party of five men and their dog team were traveling on the sea ice hunting for seal. Mild spring temperatures and winds from the north created plentiful new leads. In a matter of hours, the wind changed to the west and broke up the ice behind the men, setting them adrift on a single floe.

They did not know they were on a huge drifting piece of pack ice until evening when they were in the trough of big waves. The moon kept mysteriously disappearing below the horizon in a wavelike rhythm as the floe they were on bounced up and down.

For three days they were helpless and adrift; they lay cold and shaken and stranded on floating ice. At night they climbed huge piles of crushed ice to sleep on. By day they walked carefully toward shore where the edge of the giant floe was shearing and crumbling against the safer, shorefast ice.

The moving ice creaked and rumbled beneath them as temperatures plummeted. Crossing the ever-changing floe to the shorefast ice was risky. The ice opened and closed so quickly one man's feet were caught in a crack and the ice had to be chiseled to free him. Avoiding further risk, the party built a snow shelter and stayed put in the hopes of waiting for a rescue.

Two of the younger men became impatient with the plan and pushed on, walking all day long. Exhausted beyond measure, both fell asleep on the ice and never woke up. The elder men found driftwood on a floe and built a small fire to melt snow in a can for drinking water. Only the patient ones lived to tell the story.

More recently a group of experienced whalers and their crews floated helplessly on a mass of shorefast ice as large as a football field when it broke off without warning into the Chukchi Sea. Several crewmembers raced across the splitting ice on their snow machines just in time to escape the fugitive floe.

The sky was heavy with fog, making it nearly impossible to find the others on the enormous floe. Rescue teams finally found the men through the use of satellite-tracking equipment. Once located, daring helicopter pilots landed on the fog-entrenched floe and airlifted the crewmembers back to solid ground. Within hours the platform of ice severed into smaller floating islands as snow machines and mounds of gear slipped headlong into the stirring black sea.

Only a couple weeks remained of the spring whale hunt on the Arctic coast and by June or July, depending on wind and temperature, the sea ice would start rotting. Old ice would become ungrounded and shift seaward. Shorefast ice would melt. The whalers would go home and wait for the ice to continue its perennial ritual of change. Hoping for an early solid freeze, they would pray for a successful hunt the following fall.

In the meantime, families drive their snow machines as far out as the sea ice will hold them. For hours they watch flocks of old squaw take wing, flying toward a boundless horizon. In the village at 40 degrees, children clad in T-shirts and jeans race their dirt bikes on the frozen tundra. At the shoreline they jump floe to floe, hurtling the ice in their play.

ODE TO ALASKA'S NATIVE WOMEN

All things dance, including all animals.
Theresa Moses, Toksook Bay, Alaska

I. WOMEN MAKING DOLLS

1. I walk among women who gather at night in a small, poorly lit cabin in southwest Alaska. It is the night of a full moon, where silent whispers whisk across fresh-blown snow. The women gather to make dolls for their daughters. They dust their parkas coming in from the cold and wipe the runny noses of their red-cheeked children. One woman tells a story about her people long ago. A woman would wrap a doll in birch bark and hang it from a tree in a secret place. The doll would be visited by a shaman, who would talk to it, asking if game would be plentiful that year. Weeks later he would bring the doll back to the woman. If the doll had caribou hairs in its birch bark wrap, the caribou would come and give itself to the hunters. If fish scales were found, the salmon would handily swim into their nets.

2. The women sit in a circle around a wooden table. A tang of tallow wafts in the air; wood and leather mix with the pungent smell of moose stew simmering on the stove. The table is brimming with swatches of animal hides and bright calico fabric. One woman removes thick heavy needles from her needle box and lines them up on the table next to a box of cotton stuffing. She takes out dental floss, a durable thread. "Our grandmothers used thin strands of sinew for thread, from the backs of white whales. Now we use dental floss. Works real good," one woman says.

3. The dolls' bodies are made of debarked cottonwood, cool and smoothed by weather. I watch the women wrap the wood in layers of gauze until each looks plump and soft and lifelike. The women use ulu knives, a half-moon blade attached to a half moon piece of wood that cradles snugly in the palms of their hands. "You try it," one woman says. She slices through a hide she will use to sew the parka for her doll. I chop and fumble, my slices not so tidy.

4. "Yah, we sew parkas for the dolls. Parkas tell stories just like books do." One woman chooses a red-and-green calico print to sew the parka for her doll. Others choose colorful corduroys or thin squirrel pelts. The women trim the parkas with tiny wolf tassels, seed beads, and rickrack. "Next I make berry basket for my doll. Out of birch bark."

5. They cut swatches of fine hair for hood ruffs and mukluk trimmings, the mukluks an exact replica of their winter boots made from sealskin. Each ornamental stitch and addition to the parka represents something meaningful to the women. A brown piece of fur on the top of a hood is a bear sitting on a mountain. A swatch of white rabbit fur around the doll's face is snow. Curvy white stitches on a sleeve become a white whale diving and surfacing in the water.

6. It is written how every stitch and adornment on a doll signals a story, illustrating the ancestral ties of the people. An'gaqtar was the daughter of Raven, the Creator. It is said that An'gaqtar left small sacks of her menstrual blood in sacred places on the tundra. There the people would gather red clay and use it to color strips of bleached swan feet leather or the inner lining of bearded seal esophagus. These colorful strips represented the blood of their ancestral mother, An'gaqtar. They were sewn onto the parkas in her honor.

7. Between childhood and adulthood, a girl's first menstruation was referred to as "putting away the doll." The progression from girlhood to womanhood was taken seriously and deeply

respected. In the old days a girl was confined during her menstruation, as it was thought her odor was very powerful and could distract men from their work and bring bad luck when they hunted. A girl was not allowed to play with other children or help the adults with daily chores until her menstruation was finished. It was a special time in her life when she spent time alone as her body changed, readying itself for childbearing. Eventually she would give her doll to a younger girl who would carry forth the tradition so that *her* life could be honored during this important time of getting ready.

8. A shine of silver moon falls through the cabin window. It spills onto the wooden table, adding to the dim light of a single bulb on the cabin ceiling. One woman holds her doll in the light and smiles. Another woman speaks. She talks of tanning hides, the old way. Her mother and grandmother tanned moose hides with the animals' brains. "Let nothing go to waste." After the kill, they waited for the brain tissue to turn green. Then they mixed the tissue with water and hand spread it over the hide's hair. "Roll up the hide, bury it in the ground. Seven days later, dig it up. All the hairs fall off. Then scrape a little with ulu knife, the old way."

9. A woman cuts away at a beaver hide with golden brown hair. The children watch intently for a little while, then scatter to play games on the floor. The women's attention is focused on the dolls that become representations of their people. On the crown of one hood, a woman sews a piece of ivory. The crown is the place where the mind lies. The ivory points to an area of awareness where all people are connected to the universe.

10. One woman says, "Things were different when I was a girl. I had to watch my mother carefully. If every stitch was not perfect she would take them out. I had to start all over again." She tells the story of a mother who instructed her child not to play with her new doll outside in the snow. If you play outside before the geese return, your actions will prolong winter.

And who needs more winter? A woman gets up and ladles warm soup into bowls. Kids sit on the wood floor with bowls between their legs, slurping their meal. A package of crackers gets passed around.

11. "How many kids you have?" A woman asks me. "Two," I say. "Sleep with doll under your pillow," she adds. "That way you have lots of children." The women laugh. "Oh, and a man. You have to sleep with a man, too. The doll by itself won't work! Yah, yah, yah." They laugh at their own jokes and tease me because they know darn well my time of childbearing is long over. I'm too old. "Maybe you have grandchildren someday," she says. "A whole roomful like this." She waves her hand toward the kids with their crayons and opened coloring books. "Then you be lucky old woman."

12. The women feed their children and laugh and poke fun with each other. The women sew dolls to pass on to their daughters, under the light of a full winter moon.

II. WOMEN TAKING STEAM

1. Our boots squeak in the snow when the temperature hovers at 20 below. My lungs breathe in dry air. Laundry, frozen on a line, hangs out to dry—stiff white sheets silent against a violet-black sky. We walk a narrow path beaten down by pack boots and animal tracks, a path of least resistance through knee-deep snow. I follow two Yup'ik women on a clear starry night on our way to take a steam.

2. The steam house stands in a small clearing surrounded by birch forest. It is almost like a dream to me now. I can't place the village though the experience is etched in my mind. This is 14, maybe 15 years ago. I am traveling in western Alaska. I remember a row of spruce-log cabins facing an airstrip, a modern schoolhouse perched atop a small rise, and oil drums emerging from mounds of deep snow like the backs of big-muscled bears. Perhaps the village is New Stuyhawk

or as far north as Koliganek. The exact location puzzles, but a haunting memory of place lingers.

3. The heavy wooden door scrapes the icy ground when opened, and a warm rush of air billows out. I pull the door tight behind me. In the small entryway, we remove boots and socks and hang up our clothing on horn hooks. There is no light inside but the kerosene lantern one woman carries to lead our way.

4. Naked, we step into the heat room. At the far end of the enclosure is a 55-gallon fuel drum serving as a woodstove that hovers above a wide bed of river rocks. A woman nods for me to follow. She is small in stature, with a soft round belly, sturdy, muscled legs, and a long black braid falling to the curve in her back. We sit on a wooden bench against the wall. The woman dips a scoop into a bucket of water and ladles it carefully over the rocks. Hissing steam pours forth, and I breathe in the welcomed moisture. The women speak a few words, laugh a little, then it goes quiet. I am struck by an ambiance that surrounds them now, how grounded and humble they are in their actions.

5. I close my eyes and feel my skin tingling. Moisture collects along my hairline, in the creases behind my knees, between my breasts. The woman continues dipping and pouring until the room is filled with relaxing warmth.

6. The heat deepens. I am remembering a time when I was working in Kaktovik, and in the evening shared a steam with two girls at the high school. One girl says to her friend, "Oh, I can't wait till I have baby." The other girl smiles and nods in agreement. I intrude on their conversation. "You girls are graduating this year? Great! And *then* what are you going to do?" Many girls didn't dream of moving away from the village after their schooling. Their families lived a life of palpable freedom. Fishing Arctic char from the Colville River, hunting squirrel and caribou on the tundra. Making a home,

having children. The girl looked away from me. "I don't know," she said. "Just live." Days later I couldn't get her answer out of my mind. *Just live.*

7. In my culture, being chatty is highly valued. We talk about everything: work, family, love, kids, weight gain, weight loss, money. We talk boldly, even with strangers. But now with these two women in the steam, I think twice about speaking. I decide to follow their example to see what the quiet reveals. Or maybe not think about it at all. Just be. I want to throw away the thoughts of experts on every block who tell me how to "connect" with everyone. Dim the chat room in my mind. I know that's how we solve problems and request advice. We talk. I know we talk to air what ails us. But now I see we talk sometimes just to talk. Sometimes we talk to *avoid* the silence.

8. Another nod and a smile. I follow as we ease ourselves down to the slatted wood floor and sit cross-legged. One of the women scoops water into wide metal bowls at our feet. Her face holds no particular expression, just serenity. She breathes deeply, raises her eyebrows, hands me a bottle of shampoo. Hunched over, the women remove their braids and flip their long black hair into the bowls and begin washing. A deep sigh follows, a letting go. I feel the warmth of the room, the sweat, the deepened glow of the woodstove. I remove my ponytail and follow their wordless actions.

9. Sharing a simple elemental cleansing with two women in a steam taught me the value of being over doing. I have remembered them for a long, long time not because of what they said but because of what they didn't say.

III. WOMEN MAKING PRAYER

1. The Yup'ik word for dance and prayer is multi-layered: *Yuraryaraq.* To dance is to pray. To pray is to dance. Dance is a form of prayer, where the spirits are called upon to offer up plentiful game, ensuring survival of the people. In the old

tradition, many people lived a seminomadic life, moving to fish camps along a river or moving to a coastal camp to hunt sea mammals in the spring and summer. Wintertime would bring the families back together again to live in small villages where they would share their stories and congregate for dances and feasts. People lived in houses made of sod and driftwood that were small and partially hidden underground. *There was no room in our sod houses to move about freely. But we still danced with our hands, our arms, our faces, and bodies.*

2. The missionaries and the government took away the people's masks and songs. As if to tape their mouths shut, the Yup'ik language was strictly forbidden in school. Songs and dances and ceremonies were eliminated, but things are different today. People drum and dance with great energy and enthusiasm. Dances both old and new are proudly exhibited as a way of bringing back the people's spirit. They dance to ground themselves to the earth, to reflect their way of being, to be joyful. Taking away the ability to make music and dance is harmful to all people. Chanting and drumming are forms of expression, forms of prayer. They arise from a thankful heart. Does the Bible not tell people to make a joyful noise?

3. I sit on the floor in the front row at a dancing celebration. Elder men sit on chairs at the back of the stage holding their wide hoop drums. The men begin a song. They beat their drums and chant in their native language. *Choose us, choose us.* Their song is a plea, asking the animals to offer themselves to the people, ensuring a plentiful harvest. A young man named Maddox jumps up on stage and joins the drummers. "Long ago," he says, "drums were made out of the fine stomach linings of walrus." He tells the audience he made his drum himself out of goatskin. "I order goatskin on Amazon," he says. "It's a lot cheaper to get it that way. Much faster and cheaper than hunting and harvesting a walrus!"

4. Drumming and chanting move me, awakening a remembrance or a whispered longing. It feels as though I have been in the presence of drumming before, as in a déjà vu. Perhaps there is an ancient sound inside of us that we have heard for thousands of years. Perhaps the rhythm of drumming is an older part of ourselves that has always been present in our bodies, a rhythm that cannot be expressed with words.

5. One by one women dancers walk on stage and position themselves in front of the drummers. The dancers tell a story. Graceful hands push a kayak into the sea. A hunter shades his eyes and looks far off and away. He raises a harpoon, poised and ready. The drumming changes rhythm, beating louder and faster. The hunter casts his harpoon with a swift throw. Success! Arms elegantly reach out and pull a rope, hand over hand, dragging the captured seal out of the water. The dancer's delicate hands sway, matching the movement of waves cresting and falling in the wind.

6. The Yup'ik women and girls use dance fans known as "pretend fingers." The fans are made of coiled beach grass trimmed in caribou hair and adorned with feather plumes. Some wear beaded fur headdresses and brightly colored kuspuks (knee-length pullover dresses). Sometimes Inupiat women wear white gloves when they dance. Covering the hands shows respect for the spirits by not directly touching them.

7. Every dance tells a story. Not just stories of the past but modern stories too. Stories about playing basketball outside in a blinding snowstorm. Or jumping in your new pickup and going down to the river to fish for red salmon. Everyone loves the dance of the two cousins who ridicule and tease each other in fun. *We dance to heal old wounds. We dance to teach lessons. We dance to make people laugh. We dance to bring back feelings of joy.*

8. A major doctrine of many Native people is to be humble and honest about one's own importance. Maddox says it is all right, though, to be humble about your "awesomeness." Look at our elders, how they catch fish, how they teach us to live with purpose. Their connection to the earth is sure-footed; they stand tall and face life's difficulties with courage. They teach us how to be confident in everything we do. When you dance on stage, have trust in yourself and move with deliberate intentions. "You can be humble and awesome at the same time!" Maddox says.

9. Yupik people learn dances by watching others perform. There is no step-by-step instruction. Children watch the adults and copy their movements, learning to divulge stories in a natural way, without having to rehearse. At the end of the program, Maddox invites everyone in the audience to come on stage and dance. "Do whatever you like, however the drumming moves you." Two girls do the "iceberg bump" signifying the breakup of river ice in the spring. They bump their butts and slap high fives. Soon everyone on the dance floor is laughing and bumping butts.

10. Initially a baby hears only sounds. Rhythmical intoned sounds fall on his ear, two heartbeats and the weight of his mother's blood. He listens. The sound flows directly to the baby's heart. His body moves to it, his tiny being seeks it out, and then after birth the sounds turn into language. When the men chant and drum, perhaps powerful memories rise up in them; nebulous memories of birth and rebirth. They respond to the call of the chant and are carried forward in life by its rhythm.

11. In Africa they say: When you pray, move your feet. In Alaska they say: Dancing is a way of making prayer. *We dance to be in harmony with nature's laws, and we dance with reverence for all the ways of the universe.*

THINGS FALL APART

Nobody can teach me who I am.
Chinua Achebe

A good portion of this story is set in the mid-1990s, before smartphones and super-fast Internet services were launched in remote Alaska villages. Over the years, dramatic cultural shifts took place, as evidenced by the ever-growing loss of Yup'ik language and tradition. In Chinua Achebe's book, Things Fall Apart, *the necessity of drawing new perspectives in response to the sweeping changes in our lives is clear. Things fall apart. And fall back together again. Anew and reinterpreted.*

Patiently I watch the weather from the window of the airport in Aniak. Pockets of dense fog hover close to the ground in the damp March air. Aniak is the largest of seven Kuskokwim River villages in the area, all of which are accessible by air or water. My scheduled flight downriver to the village of Kalskag is cancelled, so I spend some time looking over my caseload, examining pertinent histories of the children I would be evaluating to determine if they would qualify for speech and language services at school.

Walking back to my lodging to wait out the weather, I arrive at Grace's place, the only bed-and-breakfast within a hundred river miles. In my eighth year of serving the rural villages, this trip is bittersweet in many ways. For reasons unknown to us, a newly hired superintendent has cleared the decks of all contract employees with plans to forge a new way forward under his rule—a bold Machiavellian shift of sorts. After so many years of dedicated work in the field with the added bonus of valued friendships, I find it disconcerting to be set free.

In most villages along the river, my accommodations are sparse. I spread my sleeping bag between rows of books in the school library or sleep on a cot in the village health clinic. I shower under cold, rusty water and consume camp food I've packed in: oranges, soup cups, and trail mix. But in Aniak, a bowl of hearty fish soup, feather pillows, and a warm shower await.

Grace, a middle-aged Yup'ik Eskimo woman, takes note of everyone who crosses the threshold of her small boxy home where she and her non-native husband raised five daughters. After the girls left, three tiny bedrooms were transformed for guests. Mama Grace, as she is known throughout the region, harbors a variety of people: public health nurses, biologists, teachers, archaeologists, and technology consultants to name a few. Short, with jet-black hair and a wide smile, Grace jokingly introduces me to her other guests as her sixth daughter.

"You're in my journal," she said one day as she flipped through the pages of a leather-bound book tagged with recipe cards. "The woman with the long brown hair." A keeper of details, Grace documents impressions of her many guests. She jots down food preferences, jokes, and stories of their travels. Curious about other people's lives, she asks about family, work, home. I don't want to forget anyone, she wrote.

For half a dozen years, Grace lived with the uncertainties of breast cancer, bouncing in and out of partial remissions. It was the people in her life, she once told me, that kept her spirit aloft. Grace launched me to villages up and downriver like my own mother sent me to school when I was a child, with kindness and a big sack lunch. I was buoyed at the end of a long work day to unwrap a sandwich made with fresh baked bread and a thermos of hot, homemade soup. Though she carried a heavy personal burden, her joy was to bring smiles to the faces of others, in a million small ways.

I'd shared Grace's table over many seasons, listening to stories of her life on the river. How every summer they used to go to fish camp and spend the long hours of daylight catching and cutting silver salmon, hanging them on spruce racks to dry, then smoking and canning the delicacies to store for the winter. How delicious was the taste of stink heads, the white meat and heads of male fish buried underground. After a month of fermentation, they were dug up, cleaned, and eaten.

Grace's descriptions of the old ways sounded ancient to my quasi-urban ear. But it had only been a few generations since the Yup'ik people took their primary sustenance from the land by way of hunting and fishing, living off the harvest of their traditional foods. Berries by the gallon were harvested every fall and frozen to last over a winter. Local edible greens and plants used for medicine were gathered, prolifically abundant as they were, in summer.

In the not-so-distant past, the culture and language of the Yup'ik people were passed on primarily through drumming, dance, art, and storytelling. Passed on via oral tradition, the Yup'ik language was written down for the first time in the 1960s by linguists in tandem with Yup'ik speakers. Most of the younger generation no longer spoke the language, Grace told me, but many still understood it, hearing it on the tongues of their parents and grandparents.

A boy in the village of Anaktuvuk Pass, the last remaining settlement of the Nunamiut people, imparted a valuable lesson. The Nunamiut people are inland Inupiat Eskimos who hunt caribou rather than marine animals like their relatives on the coast. The Nunamiut are referred to as the "people of the land." I started his assessment with the required standardized vocabulary test that measures a child's understanding of common words. I opened a booklet and asked him to respond by pointing to named pictures.

"Let's play a game. Can you point to a picture that I name?" The boy raised his eyebrows, a nonverbal cue meaning yes.

"Point to the table," I requested. "Which one is a table?" He hesitated briefly then pointed to the correct picture.

"Point to the feather," I said. He looked at me blankly. I was pretty sure he knew what a feather was, living close to the land in surroundings filled with wildlife and birds. His people are Inupiaq speakers. Though the language has several sounds and letters that are not found in English, I knew that he was an English speaker, that his grandparents spoke Inupiaq at home, and his parents and teachers spoke English. After a couple repetitions with no response, I moved on to the next task. Still he did not appear to understand the names of simple common objects.

I began the process of elimination. Before testing I screened his hearing to make sure his acuity was within the normal range. A number of subsequent questions surfaced. Was there an attention deficit impeding his ability to process the words? Was he having difficulty telling the difference between similar-sounding speech sounds?

"Point to the shoes, please" I said. He offered no response though looked down at the shoes on his feet. I flipped to the next page in my testing booklet and presented him with a picture of two spoons that differed in size, one small and one large. "Which one is bigger, this one or that?" From a picture of clothing, foods, and toys, I asked, "Show me all the things we eat." He cradled his chin in his palm and stared out the window.

Finally, he looked at me—this boy barely four years old—and said, "I don't care." Not in a rebellious or smart aleck way. He was telling the truth. My questions were excessive, out of context, and held no meaning for him. He was thoroughly bored and clearly not accustomed to rapid-fire directions. At home he is not required to perform or answer questions. His natural inclinations are trusted, and he is not assailed with questions from his parents to show what he knows. In his culture, learning takes place by watching the actions of his siblings, parents, and elders. Responding to rapid and rote questions was hollow and purposeless.

In the context of his world, where he may accompany his father on a caribou hunt, being still and quiet was necessary for their success. There is a close connection between the animal world and the human world in his culture. Waiting, watching, being patient and observant, aware of the sounds, smells, movement, and activity all around does not necessitate talking, and in fact, may disparage his father's efforts.

I thought of my own kids. How they were being educated at home, where I began by pointing and naming pictures in board books as early as one year of age. Clearly, in the context of their lives, I was preparing them for college from the moment they were born. With the expectation that they would be attending school, sitting within four walls, albeit in a highly static environment for 16 or more years of their lives. One way of educating is not better than another, just different.

Changes were made on my visits thereafter. Though standardized tests are required by law to access the services of special education, it made no sense to ask a child to point to a picture of a parking meter when he has never seen one before. How does one compare a child's everyday experiences in a remote Alaska village to those of children in Des Moines or Buffalo, where the cultural variances are as wide as the river long?

A child's speech and language skills do not develop in a bubble, independent of his particular way of life. To dive below the surface of test scores and sink deeper into a true assessment of language competence, my normal practices required change.

On later visits, I utilized supplemental activities to round out an overall assessment. I visited a child's home where, with help from Mom, we wrote up a grocery list and went shopping together at the village store. In early September, we hiked across the tundra and picked berries, talking descriptively about our excursion. On cold winter nights, we played basketball in the school gym. I observed how the child interacted with his friends, how well he comprehended directions from others, and if his speech was intelligible to me, an unfamiliar listener.

I conversed with elders, some who came to school to have hot lunch with their grandchildren and spoke to them in Inupiaq (which many children understand but do not speak). Using supplemental materials, I asked the child to identify familiar vocabulary like pictures of a mail plane and its contents. What is under the tarp of a freight sled being pulled by a snow machine? Describe where you go to hunt for caribou. What items line the shelves of the village store? These subject areas provide vocabulary words that are meaningful to the child's routine activities and home life.

In many Native cultures, extended family includes cousins, uncles, aunts, grandparents, great-grandparents, and friends. The teaching of children is shared by everyone in the village. Children are guided in an indirect way, devoid of inordinate urging that, in the old days, was thought to harm a child's inner spirit.

Verbal instruction is limited. I saw this play out when a group of adults performed a Yup'ik Eskimo dance at a large public gathering. The dancers were dressed in their traditional ceremonial clothing. Behind the dancers male elders sat in chairs and beat out a rhythm on wide, sealskin drums.

A three-year-old child walked onto the stage and wandered down the line of dancers. He stopped between dancers and stared wide-eyed at their activity. No one paid him attention nor was he scooped up off the stage. The dancers continued dancing and the child moved among them, watching and copying their gestures. The way he melded into the group of dancers overrode how the dance was presented to the audience. He was not singled out in any way. Rather, he learned by watching.

On another occasion, I met a family at a village health clinic where I was scheduled to evaluate a four-year-old girl. I set up toys and test materials on the table where I expected her to sit and attend to my planned activities. When she did not, her mother didn't try to convince her to participate. She simply trusted her daughter's unfolding and knew she would learn through example on her own timetable.

Mom and I chatted with no particular attention on the child. We pulled toys from my test bag. We put together a simple wooden puzzle, naming each puzzle piece. Mom put shoes and socks on a doll and brushed its hair. Eventually the little girl joined us under her own steam and without any direct intervention. By informally observing her play skills and noting the spontaneous talking with her mother, I was able to discern her level of thinking, understanding, and speaking.

We learn from each other, the distinctive ways in which we speak and interact. A decade ago many village children were shy and non-talkative upon the arrival of a new teacher. Today shyness among the children is all but gone.

"Cama-i! What your name? You married? You got kids? What your kids' names? You stay here tonight?"

"Hey teacher, I can count to 10, write my name, and catch a moose," one little girl said proudly. They learn our ways, and we learn their ways, bridging a gap in our understanding as we accept and respect each other's differences.

On a visit to the island village of Savoonga, I evaluated a three-year-old boy with severe developmental delays. Families in this village exercise a subsistence way of life, hunting birds and whale for their sustenance. I walked the shoreline to the family's house and noted wooden racks with spotted sealskins drying in the ocean air.

I entered the family's arctic entry and hung my coat on a peg bulging with winter gear. The odor of dried fish and game meat rose up. Five-gallon buckets full of tools and neatly stacked canned goods crowded either side of the entry.

A barefoot child slipped under a curtain that hung from a bedroom doorway, holding her baby brother. She placed him on a blanket flat on his back, and we sat around him on the bare plywood floor. The boy was not yet crawling, and his legs felt flaccid to the touch. I presented him with toys he could grasp in his hands and noted his reactions.

The accompanying physical therapist manipulated his arms and legs, noting the overall lack of tension in his muscles. We fired questions at the parents, asking if they would like more equipment for a variety of discerned needs. We discussed developmental milestones that compare the boy's level of function in understanding, sound making, and motor skills to other children his age. I asked questions about the boy's eating skills, his comprehension of words, what sounds he used in babbling. My note taking was meticulous. When we finished talking, the room went quiet. The mother said nothing.

Finally, the stoic father spoke. "We love him *this* way," he said. "*This way* . . . how he *is*."

Silently I questioned the value of my tools of instruction, the spouting of lengthy information. Too much talking and not enough listening, perhaps. The essence of this family's existence did not match that of the dominant culture. I gathered an armload of information that did not accurately reflect the family's reality, their concrete experiences of inhabiting their stories, imbibing their air, living from the land. The father's mind is full with knowledge of wind patterns, temperature changes, tides, plants, whales, birds. He possesses a deep and thorough learning of how to keep his family alive and thriving.

Was all this data necessary for a family living a subsistence lifestyle with a widely different worldview than my own? This little boy's most valuable assets could not be quantified by numerical data. The gem of personhood shining through his eyes could never be justly measured. The love he elicited from his family members could not be conveyed through artificial probing and questioning.

"We want only one thing," the father added. "For him to eat Eskimo food. We want him to take care of us in old age. Bury us in village cemetery. He needs Eskimo food. To make him strong."

I picked up my checklists and toys and prepared to leave. Giving the mother a baby food grinder, I suggested that when the time was right, she could grind whale muktuk and spotted seal meat to make her child strong. This boy's fate was decided early; he would stay in the village and take care of his elders, practicing a way of life his ancestors have engaged in for centuries. He would enjoy a fully traditional upbringing as a cherished, *unbroken* member of a loving, extended family.

Going forward, I asked parents and educators what they would like from me, and only gave suggestions that fit into their long-established lifeways.

Alaska Natives might well be one of the last aboriginal American peoples struggling to live a subsistence lifestyle similar to that of their ancestors. Local foods are still gathered from the land, and the school district calendar revolves around essential hunting and fishing timeframes. A slow erosion of the Yup'ik language and culture has taken place over the last 50 years. Old ways of life fade in the eyes of the younger generation.

An elder once told me she carried a deep sadness that her grandchildren were no longer interested in spending summers at fish camp, a time of enjoyment where family members of all ages work side by side in procuring their catch. Elders tell stories in the Yup'ik language, teaching the young people how the land and animals give them life. Men focus on fixing boat motors and mending fishnets. Women harvest and hang fish. Children play on the beach skipping stones and building forts out of spruce limbs.

"Catching animals, making food is part of our culture," she said. "A way of living that is falling apart." Valuable knowledge is lost when family connections disappear and when younger generations are no longer interested in the language and lifeways of their elders. When language dies, life stories gained through tradition die with it. As the old ones pass away, so do their memories.

I rise early as daybreak crowns the Aniak hills. The air feels heavy and cool. The sky looks marginally clear, but at the airport I am informed of heavy fog both up and downriver. Operating under visual flight rules, the pilot again postpones. Cancellations are common in springtime along the rambling river delta. The sky whirls with a mixture of ice and moisture. Breakup of the river is nearing.

I watch antsy high school kids mingle after waiting hours to travel upriver for an academic decathlon. The Aniak Halfbreeds is their school mascot. A young football player's varsity jacket portrays the design of a traditionally dressed Alaska Native man holding a spear, and a white man holding a rifle. The rifle and spear are crossed, acknowledging without apologies or condescension the combining of two distinct cultures.

After one too many delays, I make a few phone calls and arrange to travel downriver by snow machine. Jay, a district employee lashes my heavy duffle with a bungee cord, creating a handy backrest. I climb on board and we travel the flats at

40 miles per hour, the ride exhilarating as houses, school, and airstrip zoom past. We hum through a quarter mile of brush and cross a slough until we reach the Kuskokwim River, our icebound highway. Gradually we slow down as Jay maneuvers us around mounds of ice, expertly finding a way through with every turn.

Just ahead is an elongated stretch of open water, one of the first come early with rising spring temperatures. Zipping around the open water, Jay takes the right fork, close to the bank. Within moments we find ourselves in overflow. I hold tight as he cuts left and we dangle off the side of the machine, hanging in the arc. He runs full throttle retracing our way back to safe ice.

The impending flow of ice will take a couple more weeks to fully break up, but for now large patches are beginning to sag. As we arrive at the village, moist air has lifted, and blue sky presses through the fog. Planes will start flying again.

Rob, a small, thin-boned third grader, greets me with a muffled hello. His skinny arms poke out like sticks from his tattered, oversized down vest. Rob's behaviors echo those found along the spectrum of fetal alcohol syndrome, the most common diagnosis in the region. Rampant alcohol abuse has devastated families, placing a stranglehold on their children's health and well-being. Sadly, the condition is debilitating and irreversible.

Excessively friendly, Rob is outgoing with an exaggerated need for bodily contact. He hugs my waist and pats my arms repeatedly, gearing himself up to talk, but all that comes out are distorted sounds and grunts. His body is like a searchlight in a constant beam for stabilization. With each shuffle, he falls forward and rights himself, using his flailing arms for balance. Paying attention in school is hard when your body is loopy and difficult to move with intention.

But there is no doubt Rob is well aware of what he wants to say. I follow him into the classroom where he taps the pictured keys of an electronic communication device that enables him to speak, though in a monotonous staccato-like voice. "Come . . . see . . . picture" it drones, and he points to a large bulletin board overflowing with children's artwork.

When Rob was younger, with the help of his teacher, we created a picture-symbol chart so he could communicate better in the classroom. When he wanted something, he would point to symbols on a grid where pictures of food, clothing, playthings, activities, and photos of his family and classmates were displayed. As he grew older and became more mobile, we switched to a portable system by attaching a set of laminated pictures to his belt loop so he could communicate anywhere—in the classroom, on the playground, and at home.

In the classroom, Rob endures a wide array of challenges. What he learns on Monday may well be forgotten by Wednesday. Benign distractions cause his mind to wander, making it difficult to focus on an assignment. Ambient sounds—like the scraping of chair legs on the floor or a door slamming down the hall—disrupt his train of thought and hurtle him off task. His feet, in constant motion beneath his desk, are a signpost of hyperactive behavior that makes concentration a chore. Pictures taped to his desk help clarify his teacher's verbal directions so he can physically see what comes next in the classroom routine.

Regardless of his difficulties, Rob is surrounded by an army of people who love him and who do a stellar job of meeting his needs. A volunteer from the village assists him every day, guiding him through changes in daily activities that normal children take in stride. Tantrums linked to his struggle to talk have subsided. It has taken him many months to memorize common sight words, words that occur frequently in his reading books. In light of his difficulties, Rob works incredibly hard, marching through his school days with confidence and a saintly perseverance his teachers deeply applaud.

I think about what I've learned through observations of my interactions in the field, especially in talking with parents and grandparents. Asking direct questions of an elder may be interpreted as a sign of disrespect as it puts a person on the spot, like issuing a challenge. Pauses between sentences are often much longer. An elder may prefer to answer a question in a story form. Upon being told a short story, the listener has room to ponder his questioning and possibly figure out an answer on his own. The pace of conversation is slower and more deliberate with little interruption of one person talking over another. In these types of inquisitive exchanges, no one person in the conversation is an authority figure or expert. Both speaker and listener are on equal ground.

Ilarion Merculieff and Libby Roderick, in their book *Stop Talking: Indigenous Ways of Teaching and Learning and Difficult Dialogues in Higher Education*, helped shape how teachers new to the villages can best communicate with Native families.

"Today the mind tells the heart what to do, whereas in our traditional culture, the heart leads and guides the mind," wrote Merculieff. Listen and observe more than you talk, they say. Small talk is unimportant. Slow the pace of your interactions with children when you're teaching. Go outside. Contextualize your questioning with relevant and familiar experiences.

Today the highest values intrinsic to many Native communities remain the same: humility of behavior, a quiet reverence for the land and animals, sharing with others in the village, and admiration and respect for elders.

To emphasize and preserve these important values, a movement to bring back the history and language of the Yup'ik people in village school districts is well underway. Elders work as aides and demonstrate lost skills like skin sewing and dogsled building. Teachers build related vocabulary lists and weave them into their lesson plans in the math, science, and language arts curriculums. Children gather local plants and herbs. Hunters tell stories about animals. Dancing and doll making have been revived. Storytelling, the rules of kinship, and taking care of elders—many of the important elements that disappeared over time—are now being brought back to life.

Many Alaska villages are off the road system, scattered along a river, and connected to each other through the silt of their ancestors. Bringing the Native ways into the classroom makes good sense. Children delight in their class trips to the big city of

Anchorage, where they take an escalator for the first time, eat at fast-food restaurants, visit museums, and ride the bus. But to navigate the outside world successfully, children must first possess a deep knowledge of who they are and where they come from. From this solid foundation, with a foot placed securely in both cultures, they can follow their dreams wherever they may roam.

My flight back to Aniak is smooth, the sky clear. The river below is warmed by a brilliant sun. Ribbons of open water form a jagged line on the ice. From a thousand feet up, I watch a snow machine with a freight sled maneuver its way along the cracks. Changes in the angle of the sun and thickness of ice signal breakup is near. A renewed abundance of small game is sure to follow and the sweet smell of bursting willow buds will fill the air. As temperatures rise, the slowly sagging ice will soon become a river rich with another season of precious silver salmon. My job is finished and I think to the future, already missing the teachers and families that populate the mighty Yukon-Kuskokwim Delta.

After dinner Grace and I sit on her front porch steps smelling the cool night air. This is not the first time she encourages my idea of an early retirement. "It's in your hands," she tells me. She is holding my hand in hers. "I think writing and painting will suit you. Change is good. Not easy, but good."

For 27 years, I'd worked in a wide variety of settings: a rehabilitation center, public schools, infant learning programs, and home health care, my clients ranging in age from 6 months to 93 years. Trips to remote villages were most favored in that my small clinical world was informed and often upended by the unique challenges of responding to cultural differences. And in the villages, work dovetailed in a more intimate way with families. Friendships were valued and honed.

With Grace's urging I follow the call. It is time to try something new in the second half of life. Her counsel is just the nudge I need to begin a study of the creative arts.

In the months that followed I painted a watercolor for Grace that hangs above her kitchen table. The scene depicts the life cycle of her mother, a tribute to a woman who raised her children while striding through two disparate cultures. A series of vignettes illustrate an old sod house where her mother was born, berry picking with her children on the tundra, salmon hanging on spruce racks to dry, and finally, her grave surrounded by a white picket fence that is thought to scare off evil spirits.

"Look. A pholad." Grace picks up a rock from a large collection lined up on her porch.

"A geologist gave it to me. It's a rock creature. A small organism that lives and feeds off rocks. He found lots of them, and petrified scallops too, out here in the Aniak hills." She makes a wide sweep of the land with her hand. "To think that at one time, we all were the sea."

Just before I board the jet, Grace gifts me a pair of beaded earrings made by a local woman. The cobalt blue and silver beads are woven in a traditional pattern that hang almost to my collarbones. They are elegant, like the giver with her sturdy, caring presence. I wish her well and say goodbye.

One fall day as I gazed out the window of my studio, I thought of Grace. It was six years after my contract dismissal. Rosy alpenglow glazed the mountaintops as the sun leaked away, and I felt her presence in an odd sort of way. Was she still welcoming guests into her home? Had her health been on the mend? Strangely I had a sense she had passed on.

Months later, I bumped into an old friend in Anchorage who gave me the news. Two years prior, protracted treatments had failed, and Grace succumbed to her long-fought illness.

I remember sitting at her kitchen table, sharing stories. From time to time, her grandchildren streamed in, grabbing sweets from the cookie jar. Local fishermen stopped by for coffee with details of their catch. With an apron perpetually tied around her plump waist, Grace made flourishing gestures with a ladle in one hand as she talked about her mother and the old ways of life on the river.

My memory of her with an enduring smile in her eyes and the way she showered her guests with generosity and warmth carried with it a deep residue of sorrow. Sorrow in knowing she is missed by many—the scientists, nurses, pilots, teachers, and travelers who crossed her path. There is indeed no greater legacy than kindness. Sorrow, side-saddled with joy, and appreciation, too, for the way she encouraged me to begin again.

WATER MASK

This is all there is. The path comes to an end among the parsley.
Alan Watts

The women in my family never cared for cooking. My mother, feeding a family of seven, preferred the simmer and stew of one-pot meals where she measured ingredients in pinches and handfuls. She prepared meals simply, choosing items from the basic recommended food groups of her time. Rather than create an artful four-course dinner, her main goal was to keep the troops' bellies full. In fact, I'm sure she would have enjoyed *The I Hate to Cook Book* published in 1960 that eschewed hours of monotonous kitchen time preparing meals from scratch. She welcomed ready-made cake mixes and crock-pot dinners that secured more time for other duties, like replacing peeling wallpaper or fashioning a dress for her daughter's junior prom on my grandmother's old Singer sewing machine.

Years later then, it was only natural my mother enthusiastically relish fresh red salmon, caught and harvested in one fell swoop. On her last visit to Alaska, we sat dreamy-eyed around a campfire on the Copper River, watching our fish wheel make languid sweeps in the sludge-brown current. The giant wheel, nestled firmly in the water on floats, turned round and round, pushed by the force of the current. A hollow sound of tumbling rocks lulled us as the wheel's baskets gently scraped the river bottom.

We sat on birch stumps roasting marshmallows and talked late into the light-filled night. My mother was a believer in extra sensory perception and the value of dreams to hint at future events. Shortly before my grandmother suffered a debilitating stroke, my mother dreamed of lightning striking a power line, producing a ball of fire, and likened it to my grandmother's spark-filled brain and its disconnected circuitry. She believed in angels as spirits that occupy space all around us, dispensing guidance in times of need. Frequently she talked about death, always in a lighthearted way.

"I'm not afraid to die," she said. "In fact, I welcome it."

In the middle of our discussion on the value of cremation, a loud thumping brought us to our feet. As the wheel turned, the first red salmon slid from the basket and into the wheel box where we were blessed with the beginnings of a stellar run.

We jumped up and scurried down the steep silt bank. The current kept the wheel spinning as fish after fish was caught in the rotation. And then a deeper thump, a king salmon slid into the box. In 15 minutes, the wheel box was full of slapping reds and kings.

"Lazy man's way to fish," my mother said, shaking her head in both distaste and delight. What heady abundance and all without lifting a finger.

But harvesting was hard work, and my mother eagerly pitched in. For two hours with the midnight sun on our backs, we cleaned and filleted fish on a makeshift table at the river's edge. A slanted board from the tabletop sent guts sliding down into the water. Gulls wheeled overhead and dive-bombed the river, snatching up their bounty. Fresh from fish wheel to campfire, our late-night dinner was good, solid food: hearty chunks of red salmon meat fried in an oversized iron skillet accompanied by warm home-brewed beer. Tired and sated, my mother never tasted fish so good.

In my youth, my mother served our weekly allotment of fish every Friday night as dictated by our Catholic faith, the one meatless meal per week. She fetched battered fish from the freezer and served it with yellow potatoes and canned peas. Every Sunday we attended Mass. She being a dedicated churchgoer in step with my father's side of the family, but I'd always sensed she felt caged and desired a deeper connection to an earthly, soulful god, something deemed holy yet outside dogmatic rules and ritual. I sensed she preferred a spiritual life more directly connected to trees and air and water. She once remarked that perhaps she was "born in the wrong time" in history, being better suited to a life portrayed in the TV drama *Little House on the Prairie*.

She would have enjoyed a life where hard work and a love of community bound people together, like the Ingalls who lived with spare resources in a one-room cabin on the banks of Plum Creek. Her vision was a highly romanticized version as seen through the prism of Hollywood, of course. But I believe beneath the veneer of her yearning burned a deeply felt inclination, a desire to have lived in a more intimate community and closer to the gifts of the earth.

One day when I was 10 years old, we sat on the front porch admiring my newborn baby sister, the last of five children. My mother looked up and with a faraway look in her eyes, said, "I wish someday one of my kids would move to Alaska, so I could go there too."

Then she sighed, got up from her lawn chair, and began collecting seeds from the four-o'clock flowers that adorned our front yard. Dropping seeds into her cupped apron, she shook each plant with resolve, *by God she would get to visit that place and not just in her imagination*. She shook each plant in a way that matched how she took care of her family, with unwavering focus and attention. To fight tooth and nail for her children was a given, but to fight for herself would be inching her toes beyond the boundary clearly marked on the map of her life. I was her legitimate way in.

I'd seen my mother most relaxed in the outdoors, in the woods scouring a patch of ground for wildflowers and matching them to pictures in a field book. It was during these times when she came north for intermittent visits that I'd truly seen her joyful and unburdened, where she lost herself briefly in nature's great grasp. While embracing her religious ethics, she informally adhered to a far wider understanding of life that was not exclusively dictated by scripture. She came to understand, in a rudimentary way, that the immeasurable feelings of longing and loss could be soothed through the portal of nature. A different woman emerged from the woods than the one who had gone in. Her solo explorations cleared her mind, and she glowed with a feeling of inner peace only occasionally seen in her daily life while raising five kids.

Maybe I projected my nature-led spirituality onto her or maybe she had all along been feeding me with her transcendent thoughts regarding heavenly matters. She spoke of coming back to visit the following summer during fishing season, that is, "if I'm still alive," she said. Her comment puzzled me. She was not in poor health at age 76. In fact, there was nothing wrong with her physically or mentally that would preclude her from another summer visit. Why would she convey the impression that her death was imminent?

Other women viewed my mother rather oddly in her old age. She didn't drive a car, and I never heard her proclaim a desire to learn. Or perhaps my father never offered his time or patience to accompany her in driver's training early in their marriage. For years he took her to the supermarket on Saturdays to purchase food for our growing family. After all the children left the nest and my father was still alive, she preferred to ride her bike to the grocery store. Hers was not a fashionable 10-speed but a bike with fat wheels and a basket on the front to carry small groceries. She enjoyed being "out in the air" and visited friends in the neighborhood, never straying too far from home.

She rode up and down hills even in winter, and when people stopped to ask if she wanted a ride, my mother politely declined, assuring them she was just fine. People in the community got to know her this way, recognizing the lady from "back in time" riding her bike in all kinds of nasty weather. She detested scarves and never wore a hat, saying she couldn't stand things on her head or belts bound around her waist. Too many things hemmed her in.

"Go," she told me repeatedly. "Go see the world. Experience everything while you still can." She accompanied her remark with a gesture, like she was shooing away a fly.

That's exactly what I did after graduating from college. Yet after my father died I wondered why she didn't follow her own advice. She had fulfilled her role without question for nearly half a century. Her mantle in life was clear, her allegiance to church and family was written in stone. Consideration of other interests or activities outside of home was never a viable option.

While other widowed women traveled, remarried, or pursued long-held interests, when the cage door swung open, my mother chose not to spread her wings and fly out. Maybe she was lonely and couldn't plumb a purpose beyond taking care of my father, and now he was gone. Perhaps she was fearful of assuming another role or having no role at all. Though my father was the major breadwinner who put a roof over our heads, she was single-handedly the solid foundation. She held up the ceiling and walls and kept the rains out time and time again as the necessary though invisible head of the household.

Maybe she thought it was too late to change her ways, the prospect too uncomfortable for her to fathom. Once on Christmas break from college, I tried talking to her about women's rights, a hot topic on campus, and questioned new ways of being in relationship with men.

"Women want rights?" she asked. "What for? And what is all this fuss about so-called *relationships*? What does that word really *mean*, anyhow? This generation expects too much from life. You just live and that's all."

Before she died my mother gave me an angel pin with the gem of my birthstone, ruby, embedded in the gold-plated pendant. She told me to wear it whenever I felt fear and doubt. We all have our talisman—an inscribed ring, a stone, or a cross—that carries the promise to watch over us. My father hung a St. Christopher medal from the mirror of our Buick to protect his family on long Sunday afternoon drives. In the same way, my mother believed the angel pin would shield me from harm and bring me comfort in small manner.

We are each other's angels, born to this earth to love and take care of one another while we're here. I wear it as a keepsake, a comforting reminder that she is, in fact looking over me from some ethereal angelic realm.

It was a snowy day in January when I got the call. The doctor said "a massive thrombosis and no chance for recovery." My siblings and I caressed my mother's comatose body searching for a meaningful response. We laughed over simple memories—how she faithfully packed our lunches for school each morning, ironed our choir robes, swept away our illnesses with chicken soup and TV privileges for the span of an entire day.

We gathered round her, taking turns in private moments of last respects. The whole of her being was attached to noisy machines for life support, and now it was time to let her go. I admired her salt-and-pepper hair, still remarkably thick and wavy. Her arms lay quietly at her side, her fingers soft and curled. Quiet bursts of air left her lips as her chest rose and fell. Gradually her breathing shortened and slowed.

As she drew her last breath, we looked up in wonderment to the sound of a Braham's lullaby playing sweetly over the hospital's PA system. I searched my brother's bewildered face, and we smiled with the realization that this is how the hospital routinely celebrates a birth. Just one floor above us a baby was born at precisely the same moment my mother took her last breath.

By choice my mother lived sparsely, holding on to old items that were dear to her, things her children crafted decades ago like wooden hot plates and pillows sewn in home economics class. She had our names taped to the bottoms of specific objects in her home, labeling new ownership: the organ for my brother, the musician in the family; a women's bible for my sister; and her "good" dishes, ones used only on special occasions, for me. She had written a will in simple handwriting on a piece of lined notebook paper. She requested a cremation, not a Catholic Mass. She wanted her ashes scattered in the Eagle River, in Alaska, miles away from her Michigan home where her husband and kin were buried.

I think in many ways she wanted to be *free* but could only manage that freedom after her death.

My four siblings and I split up all of her belongings, one by one. We sat on the living room floor of her apartment and as each object was passed around, a story was told or a memory reflected. After the last piece of furniture was hauled away, we scanned the empty rooms and readied to leave. As I shut the door behind me, my sister turned and clutched my arm.

"Wait, where's mother?"

"She's in my purse," I said.

Laughter from my brothers burst forth like popping balloons. In my purse, my mother was ashes in a box, *she was in my purse*, and we were laughing, and that laughter felt completely natural, perfect.

Sometimes for reasons unknown to us, death feels all right.

I picked wildflowers and scouted a sacred spot on the river for her, a place protected from human activity. Her beliefs in life were not solely attached to religion but inclusive of a wider worldview, one closer perhaps to that of indigenous people, one in which the world assumes a fixed quantity of energy that flows between all creatures. Death is simply life reinventing itself. Every birth engenders a death, and every death brings forth another birth, and in this way the energy of the world remains complete and nothing in the end is wasted. She once told me she did not expect to meet loved ones in a "heaven" but would inherently fold back into the earth in another form, as a wildflower or water or clouds.

We scattered her ashes near my home where the Eagle River runs fast and deep. The river's source, Eagle Glacier, a dozen miles from where we stood, emblazoned its reflection on the water's glassy surface. In this place salmon spawn and die, and Queen Anne's lace and yarrow thrive as summer weeds. I recited a poem by Jim Harrison:

I've decided to make up my mind
about nothing, to assume the water mask,
to finish my life disguised as a creek,
an eddy, joining at night the full,
sweet flow, to absorb the sky,
to swallow the heat and the cold, the moon
and the stars, to swallow myself
in ceaseless flow.

Near the end of last year's season, the water of the Copper reached its highest level in recent memory. During breakup the river spread its icy fingers inland and took out the cutbank that housed the fish wheel. The wheel catapulted downriver, wrenched away in the churning silt along with the old birch stumps circling the fire pit and the weathered fish table where we filleted salmon into the long bright nights of summer.

This year's wheel, bigger and sturdier than the last, stands erect on a new site, free, we hope, from unexpected flooding. Like a giant clock, the wheel clicks forward with a steady rhythm, waiting to be filled and emptied. As I run cold water over a freshly harvested red, kneading the meat with my thumbs, I think of my mother. "Lazy man's way to fish," she'd said in good humor.

I prepare it in an unadorned way, butter with a touch of basil. The way she would have liked it. Cooked plain and simple.

WHEN MOUNTAINS AGITATE THE WIND

I fly because it releases my mind from the tyranny of petty things.
Antoine de Saint-Exupéry

As I fly a thousand feet above the Alaska tundra on a partly cloudy day, a slant of sun breaks through the clouds and within minutes everything below is visible. The land still exists as unclaimed space here, land that yawns for miles in every direction in an unconquered vastness, leaving no trace of power lines, buildings, or roads. From above, there is no splicing of the ground into defined parcels: it is wild and tangible, even intimate.

Flying low is a sensuous activity, whirling out over the earth, close enough to see colors and patterns sketched into the land, yet far enough to detect movement of animals in migration. Eyes wide with wonder I watch a herd of caribou glide in a northerly direction and in a wavelike shift, course east toward a boggy pond to drink.

I think of how the land was observed and recorded before humans had the perspective offered by flight. Native people from an earthbound orientation indexed landmarks in their minds and cataloged features over seasons and time, allowing them to "read" the land's spatial characteristics from memory. It must have been fascinating to see the deep etchings of valleys and the soaring summits of mountains from up above on the first flight over the earth.

The strangeness of proximity and separation experienced from an airplane, noted Charles Lindbergh, is this: "A destination is hundreds of miles away while your proximity to the ground only seconds." Stranded between heaven and earth, romancing the air currents like birds, another world exists with waves and vortices of wind creating an invisible topography of the sky.

Bush pilots who fly low to the ground see the elegance of this topography when they negotiate a mountain pass or climb to escape a band of turbulence in search of calm air. I wonder what this topography would look like on a physical, real-time mapping of the sky, ever changing and constantly morphing from one fascinating set of contours to the next.

In the early 1980s while living in Fairbanks, I took flying lessons. The Alaska landscape is vast; it takes hours to drive from one city to the next. Flying small aircraft is far more efficient. In those days it was not unusual to meet someone, either at social gatherings or in my workplace, who was studying to become a pilot.

We were young, adventurous, and eager to investigate a world made up of miles and miles of forest and tundra, with more mountains and rivers than humans and their houses. Flying over the hills on a blue-sky day was exuberant, but trusting my gut instincts was getting in the way of performing a successful solo. I couldn't (or wouldn't) put complete faith in my instrumentation, and that kind of attitude becomes deadly in a hurry.

Most forced landings, or "crashes" as the layperson would have it, occur due to pilot error. When flying in clouds or fog it's easy to incorrectly gauge sensory information if you're not truly careful. I was jolted when my observations were just plain wrong too many times and, consequently, I gave up the pursuit.

I am well aware that dying in a small plane is statistically significant in this land, and the accident rate is far above the national average. With over 40 mountain ranges made up of deep gorges and towering peaks, it's no wonder pilots get into trouble. Pair that with ever-changing weather conditions like freezing rain and snow, and you have just the right formula for a forced takedown. These are the sobering facts.

But I still love flying, especially in small aircraft. Being packed into a "flying culvert," a jetliner with 250 cramped people is uncomfortable, and there is something unnerving about the notion of "autopilot" where the captain sits back and reads a book or takes a nap (it's been known to happen). I wonder with great naivety how the beast even manages to get off the ground at all, but of course it does, carrying thousands of passengers to their destinations every day with a stellar safety record.

Bush pilots in Alaska are taxi drivers of the sky. Pregnant women are shuttled from remote villages to urban hospitals for deliveries. Environmental scientists fly to far-reaching corners of mountain ranges to conduct their work. Hunters are dropped off and picked up near distant mountain lakes in their pursuit of game in the fall. I heard of one flying service that even delivered hot pizzas, and I emphasize *hot*, to surveyors who had been in the field for weeks. Probably the best-tasting pie they'd ever had.

A good bush pilot gets to know the sky like a farmer the soil. To know where the dangers are in mountain passes, to accurately follow the slope of the terrain, to move a plane with skill in rain-squalls all require artful maneuvering. Like a bird in flight, there is a constant ad-libbing of one action after another, a creative managing of the circumstances at hand unlike jumbo jet flying where the excitement of piloting is largely lost. Bush pilots, many of them self-reliant types, can't afford to be careless or inattentive and must often rely on their own command and ability.

Proficiency comes through experience and the true grit of fly-ing by the seat of your pants. The author Douglas Adams comi-cally alludes to this notion in his book *The Hitchhiker's Guide to the Galaxy* when he says: "There is an art to flying . . . or rather a knack. The knack lies in learning how to throw yourself at the ground . . . and miss."

Because pilots with instrument flight rules (IFR) ratings statis-tically have fewer accidents, the Federal Aviation Administration tries to enforce this rule with bush pilots, recommending they fly high into the clouds and rely solely on instruments to over-come zero visibility. These rules are specified by the FAA for flights under weather conditions that do not meet the minimum requirements for visual flight rules (VFR) in which case, some mountain pilots would argue, you simply shouldn't be flying at all. But as they say, if you want the weather to change, just wait a minute.

In March, weather in the Yukon-Kuskokwim Delta can range from blowing snow at 10 below to temperate rain at 40 above. I was scheduled to fly on one of these cranky days from Aniak to the village of Red Devil on the Kuskokwim River. I watched the young pilot make a visual inspection, walking around the plane, looking at the surface of the wings, and checking propeller blades. For this I was appreciative though I'd rarely seen the old-timers bother, surmising they know by just the feel of the air what conditions will drive condensation to frost on the wings.

Perhaps he was green. He had a detailed set of instructions on how to fly the plane clipped to the steering mechanism. Young and smelling of aftershave, he wore an L.L. Bean jacket and ironed khakis, definitely not a village dweller or even an urbanite from Anchorage.

We were packed with freight for the haul 100 miles upriver: mail, cases of powdered milk, canned goods, and motor oil were crammed into the space behind us. Duct tape covered the ceiling and window casings. The scene felt a bit off-center. Calvin Klein was a little too elegant for the artful restoration of this rugged 207 readying itself to carry us upriver. I sat beside him in the narrow cockpit.

"So, where are you from?" I asked.

"Minnesota."

"How long you been up here?"

"A couple weeks."

OK. So, he was a rookie from Minnesota who'd come to Alaska to learn how to become a bush pilot. And he was 18-and-a-day years old.

Once airborne he pulled a map out from under the seat and studied it. He turned the map a quarter and looked out the window. He turned it another quarter and looked again, scanning the mountain range in the distance.

He turned to me and said, "Um . . . do you know the way to Red Devil?" I shifted uneasily in my seat.

Surely, he was teasing. I knew I could get us there if we followed the river, but that is the long way and he was expected to navigate the shortest route over the Kuskokwim Mountains, using less fuel than following the river's zigzag in clear weather.

Over the hills past Chuathbaluk, I marked our way by paying close attention to the squiggles in the river, ground that I knew well having flown this stretch of settlements numerous times. Just past Crooked Creek, the weather began to change, and we found ourselves entering a cottony bank of fog the size of Vermont. The plane took on a thunderous vibration and visibility dropped to zero. The drone of the engine that moments before produced a comforting lull, now echoed a deep-sounding drag, with headwinds at 30 to 40 knots.

Suspended in white space, as one aviator put it, is like flying inside a bottle of milk. We were in dead time with no visible landmarks, and it felt like we were making no progress at all. And then a sudden downdraft hit, and with a jolt the plane dropped. Hard. As though pulled at the end of a taut rubber band, we jerked free to shudder in the fog-filled sky, then bounced again like a bull rider.

Rain bullets spattered the windscreen. I gripped the control panel and dropped my head between my knees. Slammed again, the plane rocked side to side in a desperate reach for equilibrium. Muscling the controls, the pilot launched us upward in search of smooth air.

Though mixed with fear, there is a certain amount of dizzy exhilaration when hit dead-on by a stiff wind. I became acutely aware of the immeasurable magnitude of things, and the lamentation *I give up we're not in control here* slipped through my lips.

I breathed deeply to stay focused on thoughts of safety. Scanning the sky, I searched for a visible landmark to note our progress. I glanced at the gauges to get a sense of our altitude and whether we were climbing or descending and at what speed.

Finally, we bumped through light airy clouds, my head and stomach reeling. The plane tipped and tilted like a drunken bird before slapping down and rolling along the airstrip. The wind was blasting sideways so strong I could hardly stand up. Relief rippled through my body.

"Were you really lost?" I asked.

"Well . . . this was my first flight out here," he said.

I kissed the ground in my mind.

"Oh, and sorry about that chop," he added.

I respected his response, after all we'd both been humbled. Though a momentary lapse of faith in flying passed through me, I was lightened by his honesty. He didn't know the way but eventually figured it out. An unavoidable wind slammed us around a bit, but he knew what to do. We shook hands and I secretly hoped for a more seasoned pilot on my return trip to Aniak.

What of situations that aren't covered in standard flying manuals? Where is it written how to land on a moving ice floe to rescue whalers on snow machines when pack ice sheers away from shorefast ice? Ice floes can be moving targets, pitching wildly on a rocking sea where there are no set landmarks. Yet veteran pilots make safe landings every day. Necessity forced them to learn how.

What about areas where there are few radio beacons or landing on undesignated airstrips like tundra, glaciers, or gravel strips along a river? One pilot could not accept rules handed out by someone in Washington, D.C., who knows nothing of planes and safety in country vast as this. The late Bill Martin, a veteran bush pilot and fishing guide, clearly explained his operating procedure: "Hell yes, I use IFR. I Follow the River."

The decision to fly is often purely subjective. Regardless of the weather report, no one really knows exactly where severe turbulence will show up, when and where rain will turn to snow and ice, or how fast a ceiling will drop. Will the dampening cold create icing on the wings after takeoff? Has the fog lifted on the stretch of air between village sites, and will it close in again on our way down? The weather is often better managed in winter when the skies are clear and cold, though during the short days of December, first light doesn't dawn until 11:00 a.m. Villages with unlit airstrips have a small window of time to receive mail, groceries, and visiting passengers.

The late Jack Wilson, a legendary glacier pilot famous for fly-ing in all kinds of bad weather and still landing on time, tells it this way. When his praising passengers ask him if he was at any time lost on their whiteout blizzard flight he simply tells them no. "Unloading the plane, knees shaking," he writes, "peo-ple make you famous, not you. I've been aroused to fear many times during instances of bad weather. Yes, there are moments of uncertainty, but you sure as hell don't let your passengers know that." Competence is acquired through practice. With every white-knuckled flight, you gain a little bit more confidence, and with a little luck the public by all rights secures your trust.

Ultimately, if visibility is bad, you simply don't fly. Of the hun-dreds of small-plane accidents that occur each year, most result from inexperienced pilots pushing the weather, flying in fog, or trying to get out of severe winds at low altitude. After each acci-dent, authorities search for that one explicable reason for how and why things went wrong.

Most forced landings are avoidable, and yet when all the wrong weather conditions line up and dead reckoning fails, some-times there is no way out and even the experienced ones go down.

While boarding a double-prop plane in a village north of the Arctic Circle, I took note of ice almost half an inch thick that had built up on the wings. The pilot had flown in through light rain, and if water droplets strike the wings and freeze, the condition could substantially affect lift. This much I knew.

Before boarding it behooved me to ask the pilot what, if anything, he was going to do about it. I knew about the FAA's Circle of Safety program that informs passengers of their rights and responsibilities. I am not embarrassed to ask for a complete safety briefing or see proof that a pilot has not exceeded weight limits (another common cause of forced landings). I accept delays without complaint and always report my true weight, though many women fudge on this. I can't imagine why. There is no useful vanity worth the risk.

"Well, as a matter of fact," he replied. "I was just about to scrape it off."

He yanked a Swiss army knife from his leather flight jacket and began hacking at the length of the wings. Shards of rime ice sprayed the ground. Ten minutes later we were airborne, bouncing high over the whitecaps of the Chukchi Sea. Mission accomplished.

Some of the country's best pilots are those few who fly during the busy climbing season to the glaciers of Mount Denali, the "great one" as named by the Athabascan people. The tiny town of Talkeetna is the jumping-off point for climbers tackling a Denali ascent. Climbers and recreational skiers fly up to Ruth Glacier in the Sheldon Amphitheater, named after Don Sheldon, one of the earliest pioneers of landing planes on glaciers.

Flying in mountains and landing on glaciers require rigorous VFR skills and a cautious attention to detail. One spring I flew up with a party of four for a weeklong ski and exploration of the glacier. We flew with an experienced glacier pilot, a legend in his own time who had spent years flying the mountain. His high-performance Cessna 185, a plane capable of flying in high mountain winds, lifted us off from Talkeetna on a warm sunny day in May when the air smelled sweet with the first bursting of cottonwood buds.

A few thousand feet above forests of black spruce and cottonwood, we flew over the lush Susitna Valley. Within half an hour we entered Ruth Gorge, a massive river of ice surrounded by towering granite peaks and icefalls. In rarified air at 5,500 feet elevation, our pilot did a quick visual inspection and fly-over before descending down the long valley of ice. Just before touchdown the pilot raised the plane's nose and amped up the power. As the skis touched the ground, he pulled back the throttle, and we landed feather-soft, humming along the snowy glacial runway with ease.

The amphitheater—rimmed with a necklace of peaks with names like Mooses Tooth and Bears Tooth—looked close enough to touch though these peaks are, in fact, miles away. We heard a deep thunder and turned to see a massive powder cloud cascading down a steep and jagged peak, the first of several avalanches to let loose that day.

Knowing the weather could change in an instant, our pilot wasted no time hauling out our gear: skis, sleeping bags, ropes to practice crevasse rescues, food, a cookstove, all the essentials. It was T-shirt skiing weather in 70-degree temperatures, at least for now. The pilot started the engine, skied his plane down the snow-packed strip, and lifted off before weather conditions had a chance to change for the worse.

There are no manuals or special pilot training for landing on glaciers. The rivers of ice blanketed by snow can house invisible and unstable ground below. Crevasses or cracks can be a few inches to hundreds of feet deep, starting at the terminus of the glacier and extending all the way up to the head. With the passage of time and varying temperatures, the ice and snow can shift. The only way to truly understand and test the stability of a glacier is to observe it. Make frequent flights around the mountain to study snow conditions. Make many landings over time to get a feel for what's safe and what isn't.

Tips on how to land on a glacier were crude at best when the early pioneers tested the mountain. Pilot Doug Geeting, in *Mountain Flying*, tells this story about how to land on a glacier: Put a few cans of Spam in a black garbage bag, and from about 500 feet up, drop the bag. If the bag disappears, do not land as the snow is too soft and deep. If part of the bag remains above the surface, you can land but know that the snow is still soft and getting out may require snowshoes and a good amount of shoveling to pack down the runway before attempting an adequate liftoff. If the bag bounces off the surface, it's a go. The crust is hard enough for a safe landing, though not as hard as concrete or asphalt. A final note: If weather waylays you on the mountain overnight, you are free to eat the cans of Spam.

I have no doubt the early pioneers of glacier flying devised their own successful methods through sheer will and experimentation. The veterans pass their knowledge on to the rookies, advising them to simply practice. Spend hours flying in high altitude and slow flight mode. Understand your plane's steep turn properties. Get to know what to do in a stall. Keep on practicing and know your plane well. Cliff Hudson, another veteran glacier pilot, said it poetically: "Understand how mountains agitate the wind. Learn to read blowing snow. Become acutely familiar with updrafts and downdrafts. And don't go at all if it isn't a sunny, clear, wind-free day."

I am headed downriver to Lower Kalskag, another village on the Kuskokwim River. On a typical jaunt, you never know who or what will be your seatmates. Kids attending a birthday celebration, evangelists with open Bibles in their laps setting out to "save" a village, a handcuffed criminal on his way to town for a court hearing, or, on one occasion, a body laid to rest in a handsome, homemade spruce coffin directly behind my seat.

The Cessna emits a whiny rumble like the two-stroke engine of a lawn mower. On this trip, two seats behind me are removed and replaced with cases of soda pop, peanut butter, Pampers, and straw for sled dog bedding all herded under thick nylon nets. The fuselage is chameleon-like, constantly rearranged to accommodate the changing needs of each village stop.

I am the only passenger on this flight, and the monotony of the engine drone is a soothing comfort to my senses. We are aloft on a draft of wind that feels like waltzing or being lifted up on a swing and gently set down, rolling on the pitch and lull of soft air. The movement of clouds is reflected on a string of silver ponds below, and a flock of snow-white trumpeter swans skims the surface before delicately touching down.

My mind strays into emptiness as open and expansive as the unencumbered geography below. In good weather, flying is the one place where clarity of mind becomes effortless. I can think up there, let go of trivial concerns and just dance with the clouds and weather. And it's not sheer luck I've escaped a forced landing after logging many hours in small planes. It's the experience and skill of pilots that have kept me aloft safely as I gather a greater appreciation for the tangible mysteries of flight.

Under a bank of rain clouds, Lower Kalskag comes into view as we court a powerful crosswind. Uh oh. Bumps. Big bumps. I throw my vision out there, stare straight ahead and focus on one point in the sky. We vibrate wildly over the tops of yellow-leaved birch trees and stands of black spruce, the airstrip clearly in sight.

Three-wheelers kick up stones, and an old pickup lumbers down the gravel road toward the airstrip. The village comes alive, momentarily, to pick up food supplies and mail and to greet the lone visitor. We touch down, catch a few rocky bounces, and roll to a stop. After the pilot unloads, I shake his hand and thank him for the exhilarating, successful flight.

"Nothin' better than air time," he says, eyeing the movement of curling storm clouds above us. I figure he is in a hurry to get moving.

"Oh, and sorry about that chop."

I knew I recognized him! It was the rookie kid from Minnesota who is slowly morphing his way into a respected veteran flyer. Sure. We experienced that chop together last spring.

He swings himself into the cockpit and slams the flimsy door shut. With a steady urgency, he taxis down the strip and lifts off with a bit of a wobble, then corrects himself as he charges into the ever-changing rodeo of sky.

THE HORSE OF TEN TOES

If one keeps walking, everything will be all right.
Søren Kierkegaard

Tazlina River. I'm walking the frozen ground just a few miles downriver from our fishing cabin on the Copper, where the two rivers join. Delighted with every curve and bend, I begin my trek from a curling slough where overflow threatens to soak my boots. Snowshoes keep me a bit buoyant as I tromp across narrow sections of thin water on ice.

The Athabascan word *tazlina* means "swift water." In summer the gradient of the river is steep, with riffles and a wide channel of boulders laid bare. Its bluish-gray tint from glacial flour is gorgeous to behold in June. Today the cast is monotone. The sun beats on old gray snow, turning it to slush in parts.

I've grown accustomed to using walking poles to climb up and down muddy mountain trails, to cross fast-moving creeks, to walk steadily on ice. Mine are nothing fancy, not like the expensive carbon tipped, super lightweight, collapsible, push-button poles from the local sporting goods store. I've repurposed old ski poles left over from the thrills of alpine skiing in my younger years.

I like to think of them as crutches. Not in a disparaging way, but in a way akin to the sun's crutches. For the Inupiat people in northern Alaska, two long bars are often seen on either side of the sun that resemble walking sticks or crutches. These so-called sun dogs are thought to help hold up the sun when unfavorable weather is imminent. When the "dogs" are seen in the Arctic sky, it is thought a fierce storm is on its way and the sun needs the poles to steady itself when battered by strong winds.

Using poles helps me track the ground; instead of two feet, I've got four. Planting my poles into the ground, I strengthen arm muscles with every step and reduce the unrelenting forces on my knees. I can't count how many times I've used a single pole extended over a deep creek to aid a fellow hiker in her step-leap over rushing water. I like the way the poles slow me down too, so I can attune my eyes to noticing surprises in smaller patches of ground. Simple discoveries found at a snail's pace on level soil make a strong case for harmony with the ground directly beneath my feet.

The Yup'ik people of southwest Alaska call their walking poles *ayaruq*, which means "a stick to help you on your way." The walking stick helps to point out hazards like wet mushy spots on the tundra. I know this is obvious but read on. There's more to it than meets the eye.

Always poke before you step. Discover where the ground is firm, where it will accept your weight. Accept your weight is the catch. The earth is speaking: *You are not accepted here, find another path. Especially during freeze-up, use your stick to check the ice, make sure it is thick enough for travel. Ayaruq takes you along the right path,* they say.

It is not just a declaration of safety and common sense. To discover the *right way* is to be thoughtful and aware in the world, an admonition to be cognizant and respectful of your surroundings.

Joseph Rael, a Native American mystic of the Tewa tradition says, "We are vibration and we are breathing through our feet." I like this image of breathing through my feet. As I impress my weight into the ground, the earth energy springs up to meet it. There is reciprocity in creating both balance and harmony. Like a conscious breath serves to ground and anchor the mind, a thoughtful step allows me to be aware of my surroundings and walk the path in a reflective way.

Rael writes that when he needs answers in his personal life, he walks. One time he walked 80 miles. In the months that followed, he was given many insights in the form of images and dreams. He remembered his childhood, how he would go out in a field with his father. His father would say, get a hold of the *taa* (plow) and put the reins around your shoulders. *Taa* also means, in the Tewa language, a "person walking."

A person when walking is plowing, just as he did with the plow and team of horses. Plowing the ground, turning the soil over in preparation for the planting of seeds, is akin to opening the mind. A person walking is plowing her field and raking through her inner soil in preparation for new insights.

I imagine how poking the skin of the earth with my poles sounds to creatures within earshot. I don't see the hare under the bush because I've flushed it out long before I reach its hiding place. I imagine all the birds and squirrels diving for cover when they hear me coming.

The slower I walk, the more I see. As I leave the noise of town, I make it a point to become aware of the sounds and smells of the natural world. I feel the movement of air and hear the rustle of leaves. With ears pricked for sound and movement, I walk slowly. Days later, I write a poem.

Feet planted
nowhere to go, no final destination.
Overcome resistance, take the day's
first steps through
the bottoms of
your breathing feet.
Walk on
walk it out
walk rhythmic like a song.

Answers to questions rumble below ground, above,
the "shank's mare" hesitates and stumbles.
Keep walking
balance your energy, watch scenes
unfold with nowhere to go
no final destination but the here, and now

in walking there, where
one step at a time
moving heals all, and motor-less motion renders

a clearing of the deadfall.

Movement on foot is automatic and ordinary, but it has the potential to be much more than just a means to an end. As Thich Nhat Hanh writes in *Resting in the River*, "Walking meditation means to enjoy walking without any intention to arrive."

"We walk to go somewhere and that is why we do not enjoy every step we take," he says. "Do not lose yourself in the future or past; do not get caught up in your anger, worries, and fear. Just walk, conscious of every step. This is how to touch life deeply."

I decided to try this simple exercise, to challenge my thinking and walk a chosen route, being acutely aware of every step, like a monk I once saw on the streets of Bangkok. He walked very slowly, one step at a time. People raced around him in a blur of activity, but he paid them no mind. In slow motion he walked, one foot in front of the other, as quiet and sure as a beacon shooting through an ocean storm. The way he moved made me stop in my tracks. He stood out in the crowd. His calm presence caused me to slow down and notice each step.

During this experiment, I became acutely aware of everything: my breath, the soft breeze on my face, the slant of the sun, the weight and balance of my body in space.

The most rewarding result of walking with awareness was this: I noticed my mind open into a vaster space, I was "clearing the deadfall," as it were, where petty concerns and nagging problems shifted and melted away. I silently thanked him for opening my eyes to a refreshing moment.

One step at a time is good.

The Tazlina River meanders. I walk the bends and turns as the flow falls back upon itself, creating a series of oxbow shapes on the land. I read that meanders of this type are a sign that a river has lived a long life. As rivers age, they develop more and more meanders.

If this is true, the Taz is an old fellow—I don't know how old—but not nearly as old as the Amazon, which clocks in at 11 million years. I imagine how the wayward river looks from an airplane, snaking over the land in wide curvy sweeps.

Straightening a river is often done to force the flow of water to move more efficiently across the land. Especially in populated areas, making a river straight was thought to be a viable way to decrease flooding. But now we know the opposite is true. Now we concede a river needs its wetlands and sediment banks to naturally control its pace and flow.

In all fairness, who would like to live in a world of exacting straight lines? How bland and uninteresting. Think of the beautiful symmetry in nature; the perfect hexagonal shape of honeycombs and the radial symmetry of sunflowers. Think of the marvelous curves and logarithmic spiral of a nautilus shell, which has survived relatively unchanged for millions of years.

Snaky bends and loops afford all sorts of surprises. One time while ice skating on the Taz, I rounded a bend and came upon a woodpecker buried in a snowbank. He popped up out of the snow, shook his little head, and in an instant fluttered up and away. I guessed burrowing into a snowbank protected him from howling winter winds; a much warmer place to snooze than on an exposed tree limb. Or maybe he was hiding from stealthy predators that were higher up than he on the food chain.

Whenever I visit a new place for an extended period of time, I walk or rent a bicycle. You learn a lot about a locality through its people, and new discoveries won't happen when you travel too fast by car.

In the city of Florence, the streets are laid out in a circular grid like spokes on a wheel. I spent three weeks walking the city and became familiar with the undercurrent of its local life.

Every morning an old woman down the street carried a large basket of bread covered in linen to a small café two blocks from my apartment. I followed her to a local diner where I practiced my beginner's knowledge of Italian with a patient young waitress. As I became more familiar with the area, I branched out farther in the ancient city by walking neighborhoods and talking to people on a regular basis.

I strolled through gardens and city parks. I met the local librarian and a groundskeeper at the botanical gardens. I walked up and down narrow winding streets, smelling bouquets of flowering plants in colorful pots lining the curbside. Getting lost from time to time was part of the process. It didn't matter as I was in no hurry to get anywhere. Through trial and error, I learned how to find my way back home.

By becoming more deeply engaged with the land and its people, I was struck with a blossoming curiosity. Eventually I cycled outside the city on centuries-old cobblestone roads to smaller villages.

Bicycle! Only a couple hundred years ago the bicycle was thought to be merely a toy; an apparatus that would never compete with the shank's mare. The term *shank's mare* is the old name for the lower part of the leg between the knee and ankle, the shank, what we refer to today as the shinbone or tibia. In other words, if you didn't have a horse for travel, you were left to the locomotion of your own two feet. As the bicycle became more finely tuned, it did the job just fine when you got tired of walking, taking you farther and faster than your shank's mare could handle.

I have a friend who proudly calls herself a runner. How long and how far she runs is what distinguishes her from others in the race. Ironically, running a foot race may create the same bodily sensations and awareness as walking one slow step at a time. She describes a 26.2-mile run as an out-of-body experience, where she loses herself in the rhythm of her body and becomes acutely aware of her breathing and the thrum of her heartbeat. A "clearing of the deadfall" ensues, where heavy worries melt away.

I'm a walker. It's less important how far or how fast I wander, and I'm not so sure of exactly where I'm going sometimes, but I do get there, wherever *there* is. I often lose myself in the rich experience of my surroundings and feel most grounded when I'm in harmony with the places, people, and scenery all around me.

Today I walk the winding course of the Taz with care and pointed attention, breathing through my feet, for to touch the ground is to *be a part of everything.*

A MONTH ALONE

Spiders should be the totem of writers. Both go into a space alone and spin out of their own bodies a reality that has never existed before.
Gloria Steinem

DESERT CASITA

I am going into sequestration to learn
how to mine words from
the dark womb of night &

the blazing sun of day
with no idle chatter to diffuse energy

no sounds no voices no news no cars where
even grinding morning coffee beans
creates a "disturbance in the field"

each day in sitting, walking, writing
an unbridled horse my only visitor

I walk a stony labyrinth with insects, dust
and a flawless calm

They say when you stay in silence for long periods of time
you become intimate with all things

speak nothing unless it is an improvement on the silence, they say
in Zen

own your breath and your peace cannot be stolen, they say

but who is to say?

this is how I imagine it but
I don't know how it,
or how I, will be

no voices no news no people no cars

nothing to do but sweep the porch &
fill the water glass

utter a prayer &
draw the curtains at dawn

butter toast &
wash my hair

peel an orange
pat the pillows &

close the noisy screen
door behind me.

It has taken four whole days to settle into this vast New Mexican desert, to draw inward and compose stories of this life. Enforced alone time requires I give the rug a good shake to start clean and free of dust—to see the world just as it is, without the pull of distractions and social strains. A small writing table under my window coaxes, but I can't settle down, not yet. This landscape, however isolated and vast though it may be, is clamorous and full of movement. I can't concentrate so out the door I go.

I speak lines out loud as I walk, listening to the rhythm and tone of my voice hitting hot air. I draw deeply the fragrance of sagebrush and notice dizzying movement all around. Animals and insects are jumping, running, fleeing. A bluebird spoons up a lilting song from the crooked branch of a juniper. My peripheral vision notes a jackrabbit dashing from a small shrub at the sound of my footfalls. There is no stillness in this outer world.

Everywhere there is movement, a dramatic discharge that leaves me giddy and untethered. How to begin my work?

Each afternoon I cannot take my eyes off the shape-shifting light. I stroll a red dirt path as clouds go gauzy over the mesas. I can't take my eyes off shiny stone cliffs. I can't stop kicking my boot at the sunbaked sandstone while examining layers of texture or picking up colored stones from the bed of a dry arroyo. While leaning against an old horse shed I watch, listen, smell. Bones and dried piñon scatter the ground, a gust of wind vibrates loose boards. From near and far the world just keeps rolling in at my feet and my attention glides there, highlighting otherwise ordinary time.

I wake at dawn from a coffin sleep, dreamless. The days slip by and still I have added no pages to the book, no poems to the page. I pull the comforter up under my chin and listen to nothing, noting the absence of my husband's heavy breathing, the way he shuffles the covers back neatly when he gets out of bed.

Do I miss him? No. My heart does not grow fonder when he is away, rather it opens and expands to let more of the world rush in. Grateful for this and the way he honors my solitude, I invite the muse to come stay with me for the day or to at least give me dreams at night, a morsel to chew on.

A memory of my husband then bobs to the surface. We are at home and I'm hard at work in my studio. I am thinking of my long-deceased mother and try to write about her with an apt description, but my phrasing isn't working. I laugh out loud thinking of her spinning on her toes in the kitchen, trying to show us how professional ice skaters turn without getting dizzy and falling flat on their faces. She holds onto her apron strings and spins. I stand and try to duplicate the memory. By now I'm cackling. My husband calls up the stairs, *hey hon, you OK?*

Because my laughing sounds like crying and my crying sounds like laughing, unless we are in the same room together, he never can quite tell them apart. I guess laughing and crying are, as Joni Mitchell sings, the same release.

I want some thoughts to sip like fine wine, but there are none. I watch ravens ride a train of wind and think about kites. Kites! It's a perfect day to fly a kite. Where can I get one? It's an hour's drive to town and I don't have a car, don't need one out here.

Why am I thinking about kites and found coins and other lucky things? Because they are nothing more than diversions. A way to distract from the task at hand. I'm waiting for a sign, waiting to be fleshed out. Instead, disappointment reigns when nothing to my satisfaction gets done.

I boil water for tea and turn away from all the sensory input. Tie myself to the chair, so to speak. Begin work and stay there.

This is what happens: my mind becomes a three-ring circus. I write and write and dearly want my words to have clarity, as powerful as the viewing of those shiny stone cliffs. Instead I get opinions. Judgments. To-do lists. Gossip. Tired irritations. Repeat all of the above. The mind can so often be a prison, a trap, relegated to shifting from one banal thought to another without its master's permission. Junk rises up.

I know there is stillness behind all this insolent talk, a gap where subtle eureka moments can float to the surface. I have trust in the creative process and am married to the notion that anything can happen. That images will eventually emerge, not only through active effort but through a relaxed sense of feeling and intuition.

Above my desk a quote reads: *My mind is as vast as the sky.* Simple enough. Its meaning on a concrete level is to heed Raymond Carver's advice on writing when he said, "Write *beyond* your story." Write beyond the confines of your own narrow ideas and perceptions. Rather than write what you know, write what you don't know. Stand in someone else's shoes. But there's more to it than that.

I want to be expansive enough to contain worlds beyond the one I physically inhabit, to tap into a wider state of consciousness that is vast and deep. Endless and infinite as the sky. It is from *that* well of thought, or more explicitly, *no thought* that images suddenly appear, like flipping on a light switch. My writing becomes more alive when I've entered an almost dreamlike state, when I've stepped out of an analytical mode of thinking.

And then I remembered a rare, enchanting day at our cabin on the Copper River. I had gone there for a week alone to write in the dead of winter. Under cold and windy weather, it was a day that acted like summer in the way it made everything in my dull routine shine. I took a walk in the morning as I always do, no matter the weather. Walking into a clearing beyond the woods I stopped midfield, turned, and looked at my tracks in the snow.

Thoughts shot through my mind like the rat-tat-tat of gunfire. A chapter in a difficult piece of fiction I was wrestling with unfolded without being reckoned. I remember laughing at the sudden stream of thought, the sudden burst of imagination, and realized I had nothing to write it all down with, no pencil and notepad in my pocket. I tripped over my own feet rushing back to the cabin, afraid I couldn't get it all back. But I did.

Scratched so fast I could barely read my own handwriting. And all those books on the shelves of the cabin, stacked in inert rows—I didn't need to consult them for ideas and perspective and reference. No need to circle those books like buzzards, picking at parts and pieces. Memories were burning through pages on their own.

Disjointed memories: a cloud of chalk dust from Mrs. Young's eraser as she cleaned the blackboard of algebra problems. How my mother told me green was my color; I should wear green more often, not forest but closer to chartreuse. The clink-clink of my dad's pipe as he emptied it in an ashtray, the scent of cherry tobacco in the air.

For the rest of that day something utterly magical happened. Images and memories burst forth like a flock of spruce grouse flushed from the trees. I carried paper and pencil with me in every room, even to the bathroom. Scattered pages found themselves on the kitchen counter and on the floor of the loft.

Armed with writing tools, I got what I asked for though not in the usual, conventional way. I wasn't sitting at my writing desk, sifting through books and searching for prompts, thinking hard and forcing too many complex sentences. Instead I was full of fire for a day where the unconscious popped into awareness. I was a dreamer rather than a writer.

All these weightless memories take up so much space. I had to write them all down. Though I didn't see an immediate correlation among the thoughts careening down the street of my consciousness, I did sense a fertile connection that would require watering later on. How one thought leads to another, it was all there.

Then the fire of transcendence burned out, and there was nothing left but smoke. That got me thinking. How do sudden bursts of memory and imagination burn through the banality of an uneventful day? Maybe it was the lack of stimulation on the land. There was no color. No movement. No sound. No animals or birds or insects on the periphery.

The summer's living river was now sealed over with ice. Stunted black spruce trees hung heavy with snow, and the sky was the color of gunmetal. White upon gray upon black. Colorless and drab. The landscape was like a blank sheet of paper, a world white with silence. There was nothing more to want except to feel alive through a good piece of writing.

What then, the language of silence? Where is the voice of silence in this fluent and fleeting world of sounds? Nature sounds are rapidly decreasing as manmade sounds crowd the airwaves, even in the most remote of places. I wonder if there are *any* places left in the world free from the noise of human activity. Are there any quiet places left where there is not so much an absence of sound but an absence of manufactured noise?

I have traveled to many remote Alaska villages inaccessible by road. No matter how far flung, the "sound ecology" of these villages consists of humming snow machines on frozen river highways, the loud buzz of chainsaws cutting firewood, and the revving of three-wheelers peeling around town. Often when stuck in a village due to inclement weather after a week of work, the sound of a small aircraft buzzing the school (a signal to everyone that a plane is landing) was music to my ears. It meant I would make it home after all.

My first visit to Utqiagvik, the northernmost village in Alaska bordering the Beaufort Sea, left a stunning impression. I was accompanying a whaler by snow machine three miles out on Arctic sea ice. We stopped to explore an area and scanned for polar bears while sharing a snack of dried fish and crackers.

As soon as he gutted the engine, our world stilled. A great yawning of blue ice surrounded us in every direction. The land stretched without end, or at least a hundred miles. And what did you see? Nothing. Mostly pressure ridges of ice and snow and blue gradations of light. The air was crystalline. A hushed silence washed over us.

We stood in the cold, our faces aimed toward the sun. Conversation was unnecessary and would have, in fact, eliminated our awe. Silence itself turned into a living presence. Vastness outside creates more space inside. It was almost as though I could feel my body in a visceral way—the beat of my heart, the air in my lungs.

Mystical? Yes, great beauty is often lofty and elevating. It transports you to a sense of connectedness to the source of all things. Nothing is missing when you feel a part of everything.

What is sublime for one person, though, can be startling and confining for another. Depending on your perspective, the expanse of wide-open spaces can stir up feelings of loneliness, even panic at the lack of relief in a land absent of buildings, people, and noise.

I once read about a woman born and raised in New York City who was deeply affected by her first exposure to a quiet, so-called empty landscape. She was on a visit to a relative's home in North Dakota in the middle of winter. As she walked a stark field in the expansive acreage, out of nowhere she found herself breathing fast and sweating. A panic attack overcame her. She found no comfort in the frozen earth, no trees to block the wind, no sun to warm her back.

Loneliness accompanied her panic. There was nothing on the land to push up against, no clean distinction between the earth and sky, no clear boundaries. Just frozen hard-packed snow beneath her feet and a scary blend of nothingness.

In the city, she had rarely seen the horizon line, and it was not a source of comfort or beauty when viewed on the remote and frozen Dakota plains. The perceived emptiness and prolonged quiet made her feel vulnerable, maybe even more so than riding alone on the city's subway at three in the morning. Perhaps when we are in a silent place stripped of adornments and distractions, it is frightening to face ourselves, just as we are.

By day five my reactions to nature's nuances die down and all sounds become the music of the land. I can settle in and write. Beyond the casita, a dusty path curves toward a canyon. I hear the echo of ravens cackling, a squabble that makes up the loudest part of my day barring the sudden roar of thunderclap rolling out over the hills in the evening.

During periods of languid stays in quiet places—the desert, woods, or ocean—thoughts about nothing and thoughts about everything are exposed. In those places, though alone, I am miles away from lonely.

THE INSIDE PASSAGE

I must be a mermaid, Rango. I have no fear of depths and a great fear of shallow living.
Anaïs Nin

In Laramie, Wyoming, I check into a hotel where I can get a decent night's rest before boarding a plane to the Pacific Northwest. By the end of the day I would be joining my husband, Kent, and our friends Steve and Julie in ushering their recently purchased boat from Washington to its new home in Alaska. The four of us would motor the 42-foot Taiwanese trawler from La Conner to Anchorage over a period of 21 days. We would travel the relatively calm, scenic waters of the Inside Passage to the tumultuous Gulf of Alaska, ending our trip in Prince William Sound.

I had just finished a week's stay at the V-Bar cattle ranch. Two experienced horsewomen—one, also a writing coach—guided ten women in a workshop titled Landscape and the Literature of the Horse. My main reason for being there, besides learning the craft of writing, was to become more at ease with horses. I wanted to learn more about these beautiful animals that had always frightened me by their size and seemingly unpredictable behaviors. Learning to ride with confidence was my goal, but even more so, I wanted to arrive at a place where I trusted the instincts of both me and the animal under my care.

It may appear the two trips planned back to back have little in common, but in fact each bore a fundamental purpose: to investigate the impression of fear. Truth be told I am intimidated by the power of things, the power of wide angry oceans and animals that measure in at 15 hands and 1,200 pounds. The horse and the

sea are one in the same, like wild children spinning and tumbling.
I would learn to revere them both.

It takes a long while to establish comfort and confidence as I walk
among our spirited herd of horses. A horse is adept at detecting its
rider's emotions, and today I am to learn, by riding bareback, how to
read my horse's cues. I am being guided to feel and sense his body by
becoming aware of his musculature and breathing.

I mount. Fear rises up. With no stirrups or reins, how do I deter-
mine who is in charge? I clutch his withers and grip my thighs into
his sides so I won't slide off. He responds in the only way he knows
how, and that is to mirror my fear. He breaks into a trot, snorting and
shaking his head. Then he halts on a dime so unexpectedly I nearly
tumble off, head first.

Where is this dream, this taste of freedom gained by riding
bareback, strong and confident, the wind whipping through my
hair? It is only a dream. I am afraid, and my horse knows it. I dis-
mount and simply stand beside him, burying my tearful eyes in
his neck so the other women won't detect my disappointment.

Under the Pacific Northwest's muddy skies, we begin our journey.
Our friends' boat, *Room Seven*, will carry us 2,238 miles north, at
an average speed of eight knots per hour. We leave La Conner for
the Inside Passage, where land is always in sight, and the coastal
waterways duly pleasant up through Prince Rupert, Ketchikan,
Petersburg, and other ports of call. I push out of my mind the last
leg, where we would cross the turbulent, dangerous waters of the
Gulf of Alaska in our reach to the protected waters of home.

By way of Greek mythology, Poseidon, god of the sea, rules from his
underwater palace and has the ability to both calm the sea and stir
it up with great violence. When asked by the woman of his desire,
Demeter, to make for her the most beautiful animal in the world, he
obliges by creating the horse.

On board the boat, I note how words and their definitions have taken on new meanings. On a horse it's called *rope*, on a boat it's called *line*. Yesterday I used a bowknot to tie my horse to a post. Today I practice a cleat hitch to secure the boat to a dock. The land has morphed from scrabble ground to fluid waves.

I breathe in moisture and fresh sea smells and think about sea waves and how wind pushes and lifts water, changing riffles to haystacks, and surge waves to swells. I push fear down when I think of the gulf, and question if I'm prepared for the task.

On the calm days of cruising the Inside Passage, I write words like *mist-shrouded fjords, cascading waterfalls,* and *tidewater glaciers* in the pages of my journal. We stop in friendly coastal towns to shop for groceries and wine. A fellow boater gifts us with fresh-caught crab. We weave narrow passages, winding in and around green islands on our journey up the Pacific coast.

During cruising time there is no reason to be overly busy. We have hours of leisure time to read, draw, and reflect. There is a temporal warp as we leave the assurance of dry land. A gradual adaptation creeps in as each of us quietly forms our own bubble of activity (or inactivity), sometimes not talking for hours, respecting the privacy of individual space.

I spend the first few afternoons riding the top deck, tipping my face to the sun, and smelling the salty brine of calm waters. Most mornings I lounge inside in front of the windows facing east to catch the early morning light. There is nothing to do but observe an occasional cruise ship lumbering in the distance or glass seabirds high above us as they carve up the sky. One of the trip's greatest pleasures is how time slows.

On dull, gray days Julie makes comfort food, beef stew and fresh baked bread, in the boat's well-stocked galley. On the upper deck while coasting Canadian waters, we dance and sing "O Canada" and "North to Alaska." We read books from beginning to end in one long stretch, without interruption. Within days, we establish a comfortable pattern. The boat feels like home.

Until something goes awry. After a week at sea, Steve forms a good sense of how the boat behaves, how responsive the wheel is under his touch. But just past Vancouver Island, he discovers a glitch in the steering mechanism. He spins the wheel clockwise. No response. He turns it counterclockwise and still nothing happens. He is unable to execute a change in our direction.

Within seconds, he races from bow to stern, visually checking the props, evaluating the direction of the rudder. I put down my book. Julie climbs down from the upper deck and stands alert, waiting for our captain's directions. A potent sense of urgency fills the air. Steve spins the wheel again. Nothing. We are drifting.

Kent throws open the hatch and jumps below deck where the rudder linkages are housed. He moves fast as we drift toward the rocky shoreline.

The day appears windless, but not so. Even a subtle breeze urges us toward the rocks and beyond, a dense forested coastline where mountains rise up sharply from the sea. I pick a point on the rocks to get a gauge on our direction. I try to figure the speed of our drift, how much time is left before we're dangerously too close.

A minute feels like an hour when an urgent repair is at hand. Finally Kent calls up from the hatch, "The pin holding the linkage to the rudder has come loose." He jiggles the pin between his fingers, working it back and forth.

"Got it." He reattaches the pin and centers the rudder, while Steve centers the wheel at the helm. With the linkage reconnected, our steering returns. All alarms are off.

Steve is back at the wheel, relaxed, foot tapping in time to blues music on the radio. The boat ambles back to its gentle sway in the current, and we amble to our places of rest, back to our magazines and crossword puzzles.

I settle into a peaceful state of just looking, resting my eyes on the soft blue. Steve handily steers us past huge drift logs cut loose from a tug pulling timber in the passage. Returning to the pages of my book, I pause and think of how each moment rolls out another turn of events. Of how fast things can change. How our safety is assured one minute and so suddenly unmoored in the next.

The way I turn my trunk and squeeze my thighs, subtle forms of communication, does not seem to be working. My horse's eyes widen. His ears prick up and swivel to a noise in the trees. It's just the wind. Why does he spook so easily? Today's walk turns into an erratic dance of quick spurts and stock-still stances where he refuses to take another step.

I lean forward in my seat to get him to move. I sit tall and then slump to get an effect, but nothing works. I'm certain he is confused by the urgency in my voice. "Walk on," I mutter. And louder, "Walk on!" I feel his muscles tense.

What type of message am I sending? My anxiety flows into his body. Breathe. Take a break from demanding. Maybe then he'll cooperate. We cavort in an awkward dance, and at night I go to bed thinking: Even if I do everything right and form a bond with my horse, my real fear is the fear of uncertainty. That I will lose what little control I have and be thrust into a full-speed gallop. Followed by a bone shattering fall.

The boat waltzes back and forth while water swims in concentric circles below the hull. Motoring through a wide channel, our eyes are set on a selected moorage. We dogleg into a cove to secure protection from winds that are forecast to blow during the night. The swell is square on our stern, and we enter into our temporary home. After a couple tries, we get good purchase with the anchor and wind down into evening's fading light.

Just before darkness falls, the sea light changes. A pinkish-gold glow falls across our faces. At foredeck, we open bottles of beer and pass a plate of goat cheese and figs. Daylight draws to a close, and we are safe in our watery home.

As is typical after a late dinner, Steve rolls out a large map with sharp black markings and smooths it with the palm of his hand.

He studies its shapes and shadings and secures his caliper to the paper, measuring lengths of coastline against the scale of the map like ancient ocean navigators once did.

In the early days, ancient mariners measured a ship's progress by casting overboard a tree log with a ball of knotted rope attached. As the rope unfurled, the mariner measured how long it took for the ship to move away from the relatively stationary log. The unit of speed observed became known as a *knot*, which was then recorded in a *logbook*.

Steve is a thorough and meticulous captain who leaves nothing to chance as he scrupulously records distances, directions, and speeds in his logbook. Every evening he looks far ahead into the following day to stage the boat for the next mooring.

What is near and what is far? I imagine the old mariners mulling over this question, using a caliper and compass to map out their directions, making primitive marks on their inaccurate maps. They had only the setting sun and the rising stars to map the direction of their travels. On their crude maps, they depended on the infamous compass rose. Long before longitude and latitude were discovered, the blooming petals of the compass rose showed the eight directions of travel.

Would they get to some ending and fall off? At the mercy of wind and waves, they were anchored to nothing. No beaming signals from orbiting satellites, no depth finders, no radar. Only a hostile, liquid world that brought the best of men to their knees.

Satisfied, Steve rolls up the map and breaks out glasses of cognac and a deck of cards. I lack focus to play card games after 9:00 p.m. most nights. Already bending toward dreams, I snuggle into my bunk. The boat rocks gently and I think I hear the cry of a mourning dove, but that can't be. It is the wily wind across metal buckles strapping down weight above deck. Then a light, coherent drone, changing to hard drops of rain.

I am suspended between deep-blue water and rainy skies, tucked away in an undisturbed womb. I hear the anchor chain clang gently as the boat makes a languid spin around its axis. And I vaguely hear Steve say, *listen to the anchor chain; if it thrums, we're dragging.* But I sink down fast where sleep comes soft and deep.

Tranquil Gambier Bay, 90 miles south of Juneau, brings still, glassy water and thick fog. Julie and I unleash our kayaks from the upper deck. We strap bottles of water, snacks, and walkie-talkies under bungee cords and cast off early when the wind is least likely to disturb. Like ghostly apparitions, dark contours of small rocky islands appear. The cottony morning fog sifts up and dissipates into the high branches of trees.

Flimsy yellow kelp beds swish along the bottoms of our boats. An eagle coasts on a thermal and then scuds along the surface of the water, hunting. With a silvery fish threshing in its beak, it shoots skyward. The early morning sounds of an eagle's wing-beats is like music, an adagio, slow and stately. Paddling around emerald islands, we slip into a rhythm as our paddles shape the water in soft swirls. The day is sublime.

A few yards from my bow, the smooth head of a seal breaks the surface. Others pop up with barely a sound. They surround us, appearing otherworldly, and watch us through keen, attentive eyes. Then, just as silently, one by one, they slip underwater and reappear in different locations, yards off and away, still peering at us as though *we* are animals in *their* zoo.

On our return to *Room Seven*, heavenly white discs surge into constellations as they rise up from the depths. Hundreds of moon jellies are pulsing in a rhythmic heartbeat around our boats. I think of the days ahead. Is this a quiet period before the storm? We slip our paddles out of the water and become still, in awe of their dreamy undulations.

I have never had a better night's sleep than in the belly of a gently rocking boat. Except for one evening when we woke to find water slowly seeping into the V-berth. Leaks can appear from so many different locations, cracks in the wall, ill-secured portholes, some unknown damage to the boat's underside. We dismantle the bedding, removing pillows, sheets, and clothing. We peel out the thin mattresses and toss them into the galley.

Where is the water seeping in from? Or is the boat not draining correctly? Water has saturated the anchor locker, but how did it get there? With no solid clues our captain surmises a couple obvious observations: the cause may simply be from rain leaking through an unsecured anchor chain hole or from the steady dripping that occurs from the repetitive pulling up and down of the anchor.

Our anxiety eases. We clean up the mess and hang things out to dry. Steve is confident there are no major leaks. At dinner we laugh over the question, how to patch a hole in a boat? Oh, the famous dike story! We could stick a finger in the hole as a temporary patch. We could use silicone earplugs. Could we use the cork of a wine bottle? Cover the hole with duct tape? How about raincoat patching? We laugh because it is nothing serious. Still, we are so often in a mode of problem solving that we ponder a list of what-ifs. Most small problems have simple solutions, though if left unattended they could quickly turn into something big.

I recall all I've learned, that is, what I've "book learned" before coming to the ranch. How to sink into my horse's body, to find a relaxed and connected "seat" so it will sense my confidence. Carry me with ease. There's so much to remember. I'm overwhelmed with directions. I talk softly to my horse. I ask him what he would like me to do. His answer, or the impression that flows through me, is this: Allow yourself to be vulnerable. Ease up on trying so hard. Get out of your own way.

After more than two weeks in uneventful seas, we leave the peace of Gambier Bay, and head north toward the gulf. The day of reckoning will soon be upon us, the day that will initiate our crossing.

The plan for the crossing: Steve and Kent will pilot the boat in eight-hour shifts, and Julie and I will buoy their efforts by keeping them fed and awake for the duration. Once we entered the gulf, we could not stop motoring for two straight days.

But first, the 105-mile stretch of Stephens Passage, a long, narrow channel that is buffeted by 5,000-foot mountains that come right down to the sea—a sea that plunges 1,000 feet below the surface. The coastal waters forecast suggests four-foot seas up to 20 knots as we motor up Stephens Channel. Four-foot seas quickly climb to six, then charge up to eight. Pushed by wind chop, we ride the swells for three hours, the boat moving at close to 11 knots per hour. A small taste of what is yet to come.

Steve, finessing the resistance of the wheel, likens the scene to a game of handball. He is in constant scan mode as serious waves buffet the boat from all directions. I feel tension creep in as confused waves roll into haystacks and hit us front, back, and sideways, devoid of any coherent pattern. A cloudburst gathers. The cabin turns dark.

In the distance a glacier shines with a single point of light on its face, the only illumination from a tiny opening in the clouds where the sun pours through. We ride the channel under 30 -mile-per-hour winds in continuous heavy chop. Pitching and rolling with Steve quartering wave after wave, his concentration taxed, we surge forward, inching closer to our goal.

I am at the end of the line. Nine women have crossed a stony creek ahead of me. My horse stops at water's edge and takes a refreshing drink. "Walk on," I say. But he is in freeze mode. I fear we are in a battle of wits again.

I am impatient and don't like falling far behind the other riders. Besides that, failure is not in my rule book. I wonder if my horse senses this.

"Walk on. Walk on." I give him a swift kick and jerk his head up with an iron-clad grip on the reins.

Before reaching the entrance to the gulf, we perform a dress rehearsal in the event of a cold-water immersion. Our outfits consist of fluorescent orange neoprene suits to be donned in less than 60 seconds. Lying on our backs, we push our legs through cavernous holes, stand up with effortful grunts, and tug our arms into bulky sleeves. Jumping up and down to fit into the suits, we yank up heavy metal zippers. Success in 59 seconds. We are ready.

We enter the gulf and the mood of the sea changes. Confused choppy waves turn into deep-rolling swells, long powerful swells that feel as though they have traveled a great distance. The waves grow in height and push us along with a force that builds them higher and higher. The floor of the boat tilts to and fro in huge, lolling movements.

I watch in the faraway distance the silhouette of an enormous cargo ship, a behemoth sight, like the rounded back of an animal slugging its way along the horizon. It is our last sighting of another boat, of land, of people. Except for a solitary bird now and then, we are alone at sea.

Fear of the sea trots alongside me now like fear of the horse, though the sea doesn't give a damn how I present. She doesn't read my emotions or respond to my signals. She doesn't feel the electricity of my hesitations through her liquid bones. No. The sea tosses back her defiant head and sides with the prevailing winds every time. There is not a modicum of restraint to be had over her tempestuous ways.

Was there a big storm in warmer seas, miles and miles away from us, blowing in our direction? Waves travel great distances. Old waves converge with new, growing higher and longer and faster until they break on land or the wind dies out. If no nearby shore is visible to stop their growth, how long and how high would they grow?

Angry Poseidon is galloping alongside us now, striking the earth with his trident and dishing up a stirring sea storm replete with 11-foot waves.

As daylight wanes, we ride the sea like goldfish sloshing in a bowl carried in the hands of a clumsy child. It is impossible to sleep when you catch full-body air time. Tossed from wave to wave, the ruthless battering of our bodies and the constant churn of our sleep-deprived minds begins to take its toll.

The once highly organized cabin looks like an adolescent's bedroom: scattered sundries are tossed about the floor. A bag of potato chips, chunks of crusty bread, and a jar of Skippy peanut butter. Fountain pens, loose apples, binoculars, batteries, and books. Anything and everything not tied down leapfrog across the floor.

They say it's always best to face danger, but I can't stand up long enough to stare down those angry waves. I keep my eyes on the horizon at the top of a wave as our competent captain surfs each crest. Dropping into a trough, my eyes wander to anything nailed down to the floor, like table legs. Legs that would stay put even if the earth were to suddenly quake. My hands tremble as my breath shortens into fast quiet bursts.

I sit on the floor and find a small scrap of comfort by fixing my gaze on something, anything, and I choose the silver door handle on the refrigerator. I keep steady concentration on one spot. Meanwhile a half empty six-pack of ginger ale sails by, the components of the automatic coffee maker, an errant candlestick. A bruised but still rolling tangerine cuts through my peripheral vision.

I smell vomit. From my crouched position I can't locate other crew members, or see what's going on at the bow. Staying in one place, low to the ground and holding on to the table stem with one hand, I will myself to become like water, to roll and surge with the energy of the wind, to hold on and stay loose, simultaneously. The sea is gathering herself up at the seams, and we are sewed inside her wily fabric with no way out but through.

On the floor next to my leg is a capsized beetle, its legs kicking in the air like wheels turning on an overturned train. There I sit, exhausted with tension, and sympathize with a struggling bug.

The sky is always blue if you think about it in a certain manner. If you think the sky is clear and bright behind the charging dark clouds, behind the lightning, behind the muddy gray mix of wind and rain, you are correct because surely, nothing abides. The sea would become flat again. Its dark gray light would turn blue just as we crossed out of the gulf and moved into Prince William Sound. After 44 hours of bone-vibrating chop, we enter home waters where memories fill the coastlines of our minds. Though we have another six hours in the sound to complete the trip, we are home, where the islands and coves are familiar, where we recognize the cold faces of every major glacier, where the best fishing spots and shrimp pot sets are known to us.

We'd walked among these lush tundra meadows and peat bogs. We'd hiked up these mountainsides blanketed with spruce and hemlock. The pristine alpine lakes we visited for cool summer swims were finally at hand. The sound was a caress, a welcoming pat on the back, where the water is deep and clear and protected from the rolling swells of open ocean.

Complacency is never an option, though. Still, our captain pays careful attention to the charts and weather. There are tricky entrances to bays when our only chance to cross is at high slack. There are shallow depths and strong currents. Protected from the open seas, land is always in sight, even though the hundreds of islands that dot the sound are mostly rugged and remote. We funnel through narrow channels, seduced by the beauty of land and sea.

I stand on deck and whisper a silent prayer, grateful to be home and safe in the sound. I am more than ready to relinquish my sea legs and get back to our house in town. With 20 hours of daylight and only 4 hours of twilight, I look forward to digging in my summer garden.

That is until someone shouts, "Port side, two whales a blowin'!" My short-lived gardening fantasies spin out behind us and into the frothy wake. Julie flings open the cabin door. All of us stand silently on deck, watching two humpbacks blow thick bushy spouts high into the air.

That night, our last night on the boat, I dream of a girl who swallows the sea. She thinks if she drinks it all in, she could know it intimately, like you would a cherished lover. She thinks if she could only count how many drops it contains, she could gain a modicum of control over it. Maybe it would even render her fearless.

But on the sea, she has no purchase. She can't secure its terror and beauty, can't tame or restrain its forces. Trotting alongside fear, she takes hold of the reins and deliberately slacks her grip. With that, her audacity crumbles and for the first time, maybe very well the first time in her life, she is ready to yield, not push. To trust what is.

Layers of creamy clouds balloon up in the morning and stretch out in the noontime wind. It feels good to reach home, to walk on solid ground. I scan my journal, turning pages that show the wear of salt spray and wind. Inside are passages describing mishaps where small things turned big at the hands of an angry sea. All of them, imagined. All of them nothing more than what-ifs.

I seek some kind of anchor to ease my fears; if not a place, then a god, an animal, the earth, my very breath. I am not out to conquer my fear of the wild and unfathomable—only to rub shoulders with the hard things, become familiar enough to brighten the tiny bits of courage that lie dormant in my bones.

In Greek mythology, Poseidon created for Demeter the most beautiful animal she had ever seen. Pegasus, an alluring white-winged stallion. But when she became angry and impatient with the conceit of mortals and gods, she prayed for *herself* to be turned into a horse. A female black-winged horse, a night mare, that would ride up to heaven and take its rightful place among the stars. Pegasus. On cloudless nights in the vast northern sky, I can see it. Shining high and helping old and new mariners find their way.

EAT THIS

Our own foods are so precious to us.
Uyuriukaraq Ulran, Chevak, Alaska

Blood flows in rivulets around my boots, forming pools that hover above ground, pools the powdery silt does not instantly absorb. The big metal bucket at my feet is teeming with fish flopping their silvery bodies into question marks as they mouth foreign air.

With two hard swats, I smack the head of a fish with my wooden bonker to stun it. The flopping stops long enough for me to cut off its tail with a small hatchet and slit the length of its belly to remove the innards. I have a tubful of fish to harvest and aim to work swiftly.

Tree roots stick out from the bank and quiver madly in the foaming brown current. I look up, shading my eyes from the sun, and watch gulls throw down their shadows, the tips of their wings translucent against the wild blue. They roll and dip, squawking ownership of the fish guts I throw downriver. They know where the good food is and argue over every last scrap.

I whisper *thank you*. For the gift of food and for the sunshine. For the cool blue air and noisy birds. For the smell of spruce sap and the sound of grass wind. I whisper thank you, for everything.

The moving water leaps and tumbles, and I imagine just below the surface long schools of salmon nosing their way upriver, smelling their way to their places of birth where they'll spawn a new crop and then die. It's so simple, really. What we have in common with the plant and animal worlds is that we sprout at birth and decompose at death, feeding the earth with our compost, completing the endless circle of life.

My community is busy, checking their fish wheels hourly, making all manner of technical adjustments, like the raising and lowering of the wheel as the water level rises and falls, keeping axles on the wheel greased, predicting when the next run will hit . . . midnight, 6:00 a.m.? Who's to know? It's a finicky business catching fish. You wait and you watch. You wait and you listen. It's all about timing and, as some Athabascans say, when the fish *decide* to come to you. Everything in their lives is connected to salmon; their potlatches and ceremonies and traditions all include the taking and harvesting of salmon. The river has nourished the Athabascan people of this region for hundreds of years.

It is said by the people that the fish are aware of who you are, how you treat them. If you disrespect the great gift of salmon, they won't come back to you next season. We have survived on salmon in a sustainable way, they say. It is our right and privilege to feed ourselves from the land.

This year I take pause to think about our annual fishing activities in more detail. In Jonathon Balcombe's recent book, *What a Fish Knows*, he overturns our assumptions about how fish perceive. Do fish have memories? Can they actually think? Can they recognize our faces as we peer down at them in the water?

Balcombe tells us fish *do* have feelings, as well as awareness and a social order that is in some ways similar to those of people. Even more surprising is the scientific research that has shown that fish display tool use at the level of a 10-month-old baby.

Tool use points to the development of a growing intelligence. If a baby sees an interesting toy on a blanket and the toy is out of reach, she may crawl after it, or she may simply pull on the edge of the blanket to bring the toy nearer where she can easily grab it. She uses the blanket as a tool to secure the toy.

The same has been observed in the tuskfish as evidenced by the biologist Giacomo Bernardi. While diving he observed a tuskfish spit water at a clam buried in the sand. When the clam became visible the fish picked it up in its mouth and carried it to a large rock, a good 30 yards away. The fish flicked its head to smash open the clam against the rock. This sequence of behaviors was observed over and over again until the fish was finished with its plentiful dinner.

Birds have been observed taking tool use even a step further. Ravens will often drop nuts onto the pavement of a busy intersection and wait for car wheels to crack them open. When the light changes to red and traffic stops momentarily, the ravens swoop down and pick up their meaty remnants, just like that.

It had never occurred to me that fish might also exercise a variety of so-called thinking skills. They reportedly enjoy different kinds of music, display distinct personalities, and feel physical pain. I'm careful though in assigning the word suffer to fish as some biologists do. Sensory pain is one thing but suffering denotes another layer of psychological thought placed on top of the pain, creating more misery. I'm willing to bet we humans have cornered that type of pain. When there is no judgment overlaying the sensations, pain is just pain.

Can fish become depressed with the state of their lot? Studies have actually shown that salmon farms naturally have "dropout" fish, growth-stunted fish that float lifelessly at the surface of the farming ponds. These fish are severely depressed. Why? Because they have given up on life. Their brain chemistry and behavior mimic those of other animals with documented depression. And they are smaller in size due to "failure to thrive," like human babies who experience stunted growth in the absence of love and affection.

Should we abstain from eating fish because we cause them unpleasant deaths? Should sport fishing with lures be banned? Some suggest sport fishing be stopped because it amounts to playing with your food. When fish are caught for reasons other than sustenance, say, for the thrill of the catch, does this not disrespect the animal and cause unnecessary pain? If we do indeed have a moral obligation to assure a pleasant death for fish (and other animals), maybe we should prohibit their killing and never eat them, as some researchers propose.

We take great measure to assure a comfortable death for humans by way of hospice and palliative care, providing relief from the painful symptoms of serious illnesses. How then should we treat our fellow winged, gilled, and four-legged creatures?

Those who adhere to veganism abhor the violence surrounding the killing of animals of any kind. A healthier, more compassionate way to live is to avoid harvesting and using any type of animal products. No meat, cheese, eggs, milk, crustaceans, fish, leather, fur, or their by-products.

Many are confident the rest of society will eventually wake up to veganism and right their erroneous thinking on the subject by divorcing themselves from all things animal.

Maybe there is something to learn from the lifeways of indigenous people; people who may view the taking of animals as neither exploitation nor cruelty. This worldview points to the animal as being in a symbiotic and spiritual relationship with the human; one dies for the express purpose of giving life to another. We humans don't walk outside the circle of life and peer at the specimens contained within. We are an essential spoke in the wheel, beginning with the rather violent act of birth. As we progress through our lives, we learn to co-exist with all of life's inevitable pain and suffering. At the end, death is not an outrage, no matter how peaceful or terrifying the experience turns out to be. It is simply the last cycle in the great wheel of life.

Many unique cultures around the world inhabit a way of life that is crucially defined by the landforms they inhabit. The food sources of many Alaska Natives are inherently tied to the mountains, oceans, valleys, and rivers on which they live and depend. Hunting and gathering and eating traditional food connects people to the animals, to the land, and to each other.

Children learn important lessons growing up in a family that practices a subsistence way of life. They learn patience and humility by listening to their grandparents tell stories of the past. Reverence and responsibility are learned when children work side by side with family members. From an early age, they are encouraged to share and are given the job of delivering the first catch of fish to the elders and people with disabilities in their village.

Food is not just food but medicine, to the body and the soul. To quote Uyuriukaraq Ulran's words: "Eating foreign foods day after day our spirit seems to become hungry for that relationship to the land; we depend on the land. Without it, we seem nil."

Should the Inupiat people be prohibited from taking whale, the lifeblood of their people? Taking away their indigenous foods is exactly how failure to thrive and depression would show up in the people who respect and give thanks to their fellow creatures for granting them life. In all practicality, eating greens at 40 below in the vast, treeless landscape of northern Alaska will not sustain you. Though the skin and the blubber of the bowhead will.

If you were wearing a white scarf, a white ribbon, or a white bandana at Katie John's celebration of life, you were one of her grandchildren, great-grandchildren, or great-great-grandchildren.

I drove from our cabin in Tazlina to the village of Mentasta to take part in Katie's memorial. In June there was still a thin layer of ice skirting Mentasta Lake. A line of cars bending east at the Tok Cutoff preceded me on the otherwise lonely highway. Ahtna people from dozens of neighboring villages, as well as people from around the world, came to celebrate her remarkable life.

Born in Slana, Alaska, in 1915, Katie married Mentasta Traditional Athabascan chief Fred John, with whom she had 14 children. Katie and her husband taught their children the traditional ways of living off the land. They emphasized the value of respecting elders and honoring the ways of their family's ancestors. Remarkably, Katie and her husband cared for their family without ever accepting a penny of welfare.

Katie John's legacy could be traced all the way back to 1964, when the State of Alaska prohibited the taking of salmon from her traditional fish camp. A series of lawsuits were put into play, and Katie gained fame as the lead plaintiff. Her legal actions polarized public opinion between those who believed she was entitled to take salmon from her traditional land and those who argued the taking of salmon amounted to special treatment. Demonstrators in Anchorage proudly marched for her, with signs saying, "Don't mess with Katie."

For decades, Katie fought the subsistence ruling. Suits bounced back and forth; new laws were brought to the table. Katie never stopped working for her people, and she had absolutely no fear of conflict with bureaucrats. In time, a ruling from the Ninth District Court of Appeals was brought forth. Alaska Native fishing and hunting rights would be protected. The long and harrowing fight was over. Katie's stubbornness had paid off.

For her tireless energy and determination, Katie was awarded an honorary law degree from the University of Alaska. No one before her had stood up to the federal government and the State of Alaska like she did—all because she believed in the right to feed her people. News of her legal battle spread and inspired indigenous peoples from all corners of the globe who vowed to walk in her footsteps to proclaim their own subsistence rights. Katie passed away at the age of 97, 10 years after the ruling that made her famous.

Without a doubt, the consumption of traditional foods is key to a culture's preservation and affects the mental, physical, and spiritual health of its people. Should those who harvest natural food from the land and water eat artificial instead, like shrink-wrapped meat substitutes? Imitation crabmeat made of fillers, fake flavoring, and dyes?

I only skim the surface of this subject. Like the gulls wheeling over my fish table, I'm suspended in this literal world above water, unable to dive deep enough to fully comprehend the life-giving secrets of how we are so deeply connected to the food we eat.

But I think I understand what is true for many. Red salmon harvested from the breathing waters of the Copper River is a great gift, representing so much more than a "commodity" or a "resource." It comes with an energy that inexplicably ties me to the natural world. An aliveness that is absent in modern, over-processed food products found in our grocery store aisles.

What I do know is life and death spring forth from this land simultaneously. Hunters and fisherman have taught me, through example, how deeply a people can believe in the sacredness of life and death. When you take away venerated foods, you potentially destroy a vivid and unique culture. You destroy worldviews in which people do not dictate "right" living to others but live their lives as people who clearly see and appreciate their rightful place not only *in* the world, but *born of it*, as interconnecting links to the rest of the world and all things in it.

What do we do when considering the inner lives of plants? In *What a Plant Knows*, David Chamovitz reports that plants, too, have feelings and the act of uprooting them causes pain. Plants prefer listening to the melodies of Bach over the rock guitar riffs of Led Zeppelin. The failure to thrive in plants can be deterred by talking to them lovingly, every day. They, too, he says, are well aware of their surroundings.

As we develop a more enlightened view on the fish, plants, and animals of our world, I wonder: When all is said and done, what then, shall we eat?

RECALIBRATION

If the sun and moon should ever doubt,
they would immediately go out.
William Blake

The first glint of sunlight peeps over the line where snow meets silver cast sky. It is two minutes to noon and light is tapping on the windows. The busyness of the day comes to a halt. Office workers crowd around doorways. Doctors lay down their stethoscopes and watch from hospital windows. People step outside in the frigid cold to witness the sunrise. It's the 23rd day of January, and Utqiagvik hasn't seen the sun since mid-November.

For the first few days her appearance is a tease, lasting only an hour or so. But with each passing week she throws down a rope of hope, warming eager, upturned faces. Like a red rubber ball, the sun marks time on sheet music, skipping across the horizon to the tune of jubilance and laughter from all sullen creatures below.

We made it.
To hell with the poetry of shadow.
Enough of dim half-light in the middle of the afternoon.
Here comes the sun.

In the days that follow, the sun will pull out all stops to flip night into day, rising higher and staying longer until there is barely a break in illumination at all.

Where I live—in Eagle River, 720 miles south of Utqiagvik—the staccato hiccup of changes in light are less pronounced than above the Arctic Circle. Still, darkness will always be endemic here. After decades of living with radical seasonal shifts, I've learned what works best to ease the bluesy changes in my mood. I step outside, don my headlamp, and immerse myself in the bottomless dark, poling my way up mountain trails where, if I'm lucky, a soft net of light is thrown down by the moon.

The return of light for circumpolar people is clearly business as usual. Years ago, there were no street lights in the villages and children played outside by the light of a bright moon. You don't miss something that you've never had. If you don't know that anyone else has the sun, you don't think of it as being a hardship or lack.

To the Kalaallit indigenous people of Greenland, legend goes that the sun and moon were brought into play by a series of events that occurred between a brother and sister of the tribe. Malina, representing the sun, rules the skies of the Arctic people. Her brother, Anningan, is the ruler of the moon. Together, they lived and played peacefully in the years of their youth.

As was customary when children grew beyond adolescence in the tribes of the Far North, they came to live apart in separate lodges for men and women. One night, it was told, Anningan entered the women's lodge and attempted to make love to his sister, whom he deeply cherished. His desire was to remain near her forever.

A fight ensued where a seal-oil lamp was knocked over, soiling Malina's hands with black soot. She fought her brother's advances by smudging ashes in his eyes and blackening his face with her oily hands. Up off the ground she leaped, running high into the sky as far away from her brother as possible. She settled above the earth and became the sun, brilliantly burning with heat and great light. Anningan, too, leaped up from the ground and soared briskly toward the heavens. Though he became bright, his temperament was cool and never offered warmth. Anningan loved his sister and chased her endlessly, showing no remorse for his reproachable behavior.

He continues to chase her today, as the ruler of the moon. Anningan's concentration on pursuing his sister is so great, he forgets to take in food and becomes skinny, gradually thinning like a waning moon. To satisfy his hunger, he disappears for three days each month, during the new moon, to eat his fill. He then returns full, as a gibbous moon, to chase his sister once again.

Malina wants nothing more than to stay far away from her brother. But he keeps chasing her in an endless loop across a star-struck sky.

When I was a child, around nine years old, I was caught in an unexpected moment of brilliance one dreary summer day. The experience was my first real memory of how quickly light can alter mood, how the energies of splintered sunlight can so powerfully change an experience from peace to fear in a matter of moments.

My mother packed me a lunch, and I crossed the schoolyard to the nearby woods to an old oak tree, one I had climbed many times before to observe the world from a different point of view. The dull sky was crumpled with gray clouds. I climbed up, hand over hand, branch by branch, holding my sack lunch between my teeth and stopping every so often to take in the view. I got comfortable on a high branch and rested my back against the main trunk.

From far above, I scanned the wide, flat landscape below, taking note of our ranch-style home tucked neatly in a nearby subdivision. I could see my elementary school, surrounded by trees and fenced playgrounds. From my school's baseball diamond, I heard the distant sound of kids scrambling around its bases.

High up in a canopy of oak leaf, I unfolded my sandwich from its waxed paper wrapping and took a few bites. Oddly, the tree began shaking. I gripped the trunk and held on tight. A hard wind blew my hair in tangles and for a few seconds I lost my balance. My sandwich tumbled to the ground. I sat up, stiffened and startled. What if I can't get down? Tears rushed my eyes. Pressing my cheek against the cool bark, I tightened my grip.

The noisy leaves spun on their spindly stems. Gusts of wind whistled past my head, weaving their way through the arms of descending branches. Just as suddenly, gray clouds opened and sunlight burst forth, pouring like liquid gold through the foliage. My vision went from gray to green. Colors popped. The opaque sky brightened.

I felt warmth on my face and arms and laughed out loud at this strange and sudden turn of events. Sunlight braised the leaves, the wind died, and I leaned back into the safety of the old oak's arms. First gray, dull sky then sunlight—I felt the joy of simply being alive. Cold and afraid one moment, warmed by light and color the next.

Novelist and poet D. H. Lawrence wrote, "In the magnificent fierce morning of New Mexico, one *sprang* awake; a new part of the soul woke up suddenly and the old world gave way to the new."

I believe Lawrence was referring to light as the key source of inspiration drawing artists, writers, and travelers to the New Mexico landscape. The first time I experienced Abiquiu's landscape, I felt like I had come home, that I deeply belonged there, with as great a force as belonging to Alaska. Both places are epic in their grandeur; both are a study in light. In their own unique ways, each delivers an intensity of perception unrivaled by other places.

Yearly I retreat to the high desert of Abiquiu when Alaska skies go gray. Our customary winter snowfalls have been, in recent years, eclipsed by weeks of freezing rain. The grayness digs in under your skin, the moon having no snow to reflect its silvery light.

In the Southwest, there is a mystical charm to how light dances on adobes at sunrise, creating sharp shadows. So too the pure light of dawn creates a clean outline of mountains and boulders. I've heard the dawn described as the most "real" time of day, before the glaring haze and heat of the day sets in.

The light wavers with such exactness, I find myself chasing it at all hours of the night and day, camera slung around my neck, lenses and snack bars pouring out of my pockets, and a bottle of water dangling from a snap ring clipped to my belt. Before 6:00 a.m. and after 4:00 p.m., I chase the light and discover a whole new world of texture, color, and shadow. I pursue as if I were gathering light itself, as if it were something you could scoop into a big clay pot and carry back home with you. But indeed, it does feel that way. Over the course of a couple months I am brightened and energized, bent on winging the precious cargo back home to carry me through the rest of the winter.

One night I went on a search for the great Rio Grande River gorge to experience how the moon casts shadows on the river. I had never been there before, certainly not after dark, but I was intrigued by the full moon, wondering how it would play out on moving water. Descending rapidly from the mesa in my rental car, I wound down a narrow dusty road bordered heavily with sage, following the explicit directions given me by a fellow traveler. With windows rolled down, I savored the night's sweet aroma of weed and piñon. Gradually the route began to climb up, twisting and turning around the shadows of sketchy juniper trees. Deep ruts ran beneath my wheels, and my progress slowed to a crawl.

Ah. The sound of rushing water. I found the gorge. The river was fast and deep, and I thought I heard music tumbling from its depths. Like the sounds of many instruments blending into one fine resonant song played by a jumble of rocks and swift water.

Standing on the bank, the typical background fear of being alone in the dark disappeared. The moon shone like a high beam on the river's percolating current. Points of silver light leapt on curls of heavy waves. It was like I had unfastened a clasp and opened a box where the luster of the moon and stars rose up and scattered into tiny jewels.

I was far from feeling alone. The moon's cold light spread into a gathering of all the elements: water, earth, stone, sky and stars— their entirety conspired to remind me of a simple passage by Aldous Huxley I'd memorized years ago: "It's dark because you are trying too hard. Lightly, child, lightly."

The earth moves around the sun ever so slowly in its annual journey of circumnavigation. In Alaska we celebrate the solstices, both winter and summer because light—the presence and absence of—is so central to our way of living. The word *solstice* means "sun standing." It's as if the sun's presence lists toward a tipping point, stands still momentarily, and then its energy swings one way or the other, like the weighted pendulum on a clock.

For thousands of years, people across all ancient cultures have celebrated the spring equinox, a time of fertility and rebirth of life and energy. The word *equinox* means "equal night," when night and day are of equal length.

River ice holds fast in our town during the lengthening days of the spring equinox. Old snow blankets the ground, the sun reaches even higher in the sky, and we all yearn for the coming of summer, but not quite so fast. Our annual spring river party occurs on March 21 and officially marks the shedding of winter, though winter activities are still the main attraction.

We ski a hard-packed trail to the river, pulling sleds piled high with coolers of food and beer, lawn chairs, ice skates, folding tables, and a guitar or two. Mamas haul their babies on their backs. A few brave ones ride their bicycles with fat studded tires onto the ice. A pack of dogs follows us in, nipping our heels, eager to be harnessed for the neighborhood kids' dogsled rides.

Conditions on the river change every year depending on precipitation and temperature. Some years, when the ice is smooth and glassy, a lively day of skating is enjoyed. Or shuffleboard, where we etch lines into the ice with food coloring and cut discs of play from the ends of downed spruce logs. Other years, heavy snowfall makes for perfect dogsled races. No matter the weather, we dress accordingly and switch up activities to meet the day's calling. We stand around a campfire, roasting chicken and hotdogs. For dessert, the kids shake, rattle, and roll a sealed ball filled with sugar, cream, and rock ice, turning the concoction into vanilla ice cream, shared on crunchy sugar cones. There is cause to be celebratory. We can feel the sun on our faces, its radiance no longer just a wish or a dream.

It isn't until the first week of April I hear the neighbor's children pull their bicycles out of storage and cruise the road in front of our house. The tinkling sound of chimes on the wind meanders through heavily treed yards. A layer of ice that shellacs my flowerbeds is thawing. I hear a neighbor's chainsaw clearing cottonwood branches before his mountain view becomes shrouded in a cloak of shiny leaves. I hear the trickle of snowmelt from rooftops.

People are out walking their dogs, going for long runs, smiling. Yes, smiling. We made it, one more winter. Here we are, fresh and clean as crisp blue sheets waving in the wind. All of us rising up on a gust.

The pendulum releases and bows toward light until the summer solstice on June 21, the longest day of the year. This day the earth's axis of rotation points toward the sun. The midsummer sun hooks you with a constant radiance you never want to end.

Like the Tewa Indian boy who set out on a mythical journey to stop the sun from setting, northerners want to lasso its brilliance and make it hold tight to the sky. Plaster it up with both hands. Make it stay. We're wooed by its life-giving power, sharply aware of its emergence and exit in our everyday lives.

But you can't push a river. You can't force your wishes or make anything stay. You must simply wait. The quack grass that reaches my knees rolls in the wind like waves of green seafoam. Fireweed shoots of deep fuchsia point their tips toward the sky. Light is chasing every leaf, stem, and seed, doing an illustrious job of pulling up life by its britches with or without my well-intentioned efforts.

June days are long and light-filled way past the midnight hour. Except for funerals and weddings, I rarely leave Alaska in the summer. I stay home where the light is bright and protracted. Because I don't want to miss an ounce of daylight.

A bit of frenzy rides on the coattails of summer. I remind myself there is no need to rush; there are 18 hours of light to secure the day. With so much light my list of yard chores grows: pulling weeds, mixing dirt, stringing up raspberry bushes, removing stumps from last year's cull. I'm eager to start new projects and finish the old ones.

I pull out seed packets purchased in early spring and thrill in the planting of heritage foods with names like Ruby Queen beets and Scarlet Dragon carrots—cosmic-colored root vegetables that survive well in cold climates. They share my garden space with lettuce, basil, and lemon mint.

While digging my hands into the soil I realize that I, too, have been thirsty for the feel of warm black earth, for the anticipation of setting into motion the sprouting of seeds and unfurling of leaves. Step aside darkness. Sunlight is barging in to reclaim its rightful place, peering through clouded windows that scream *wash me*, and penetrating the patient, long-awaited soil of my garden.

I watch a raven perched atop a spruce tree calling to his buddies. *Let's go play on this riptide of wind* and they join and split and roll, slicing the sky in full swing. From the garden, I stand quietly looking at Eagle Glacier, still snow covered in the distant valley. The river's slow milky-gray current snakes the valley floor in its own time, no rush to get to the ocean. I take a deep breath and concede the same. The garden will wait for me and everything will get done, bit by bit, over these radiant days. All the wild things will soon be out in full bloom.

I am sitting next to the woodstove, eating an apple on the morning of December 21. It is the winter solstice, the day each year with the least light, the day when the earth's axis of rotation points away from the sun. The solar path is boldly shrinking; at 10:00 a.m. it is still dark outside. I think of this time as a period of incubation, when energy is predictably lower. It's a time of drawing inward and following the natural bend of things, easing through the blue days of twilight.

We string white lights on houses and trees in the beginning of October in my neighborhood, when natural light is tiptoeing away, oh so quietly. My son's favorite Christmas, the one he remembers most, is when our home went dark during a two-day power outage caused by heavy snowfall. That Christmas we heated water for tea on the woodstove and ate cold turkey sandwiches for dinner. Opening gifts by candlelight added a modicum of mystery and charm.

CJ Muchhala's poem "Moths" illustrates how we instinctively move toward light, how we yearn for that tiny mustard seed of brilliance to launch us out of winter's prying fingers. I invite you to read it, slowly, and then again:

I am writing to tell you about the moths
Battened on the windows,
Their dusty wings outlined
In the absence of light,
Their furry bodies yearning for the glowing coals I tend.
Over time, they learn calm
Press warm and pulsing centers to the glass.
Be still, they seem to say.
Let light catch you.
Some never catch on
And beat their wings ragged.

Like a winter moth, wingless and flightless, I rustle in the dark ground of December. Though stunted, life is not over yet, just sleeping for a while. A friend gives me good advice. "Jump into the darkness," she says. "Something new is bound to emerge."

It is no wonder the winter months are a most productive time when I'm holed up, searching for words, and capturing images in the lowest of light. I pull darkness around me like a thick sweater. I track the scent and movement of storylines previously unattended and ask questions to reveal their narrative. It is a way of recalibrating, finding and trusting the high value in darkness and using it to my advantage. All that's unrealized will surely bubble to the surface. The moon and stars will fall out of the box if I open the lid and take a peek.

Maybe we don't have to search for the light or beat our wings ragged. The ground softens. Life emerges on its own. Poof! Like a seedpod it lifts off and twirls, leaving shadow far, far behind.

COLD DEPARTURES

Nothing changes. The bones of the mammoth are still in the earth.
Adrienne Rich

I land in Kaktovik, a village on a small barrier island in the Beaufort Sea. This far north the sun doesn't set between May and August, yet the ground is still frozen and tenacious snowdrifts cling to the sides of buildings. It is a polar day in mid-May.

An elderly woman named Ida meets me at the airstrip. "We are Inupiat people," she says. Strands of black hair poke out from the polar bear ruff framing her plump rosy cheeks. Gently she tugs off my mitten in the cold air and shakes my hand. "This is how we greet. Warm skin to warm skin."

I am soothed by her kind gesture. Hefting my duffle onto a humming snow machine, Ida directs the driver to my lodging at the Waldo Arms. The Arms is a jumbled mix of mobile homes and abandoned shipping containers stitched together by plywood framing. Though unconventional, the rooms are small and clean. For dinner I have a meal meant to put meat on your bones, cheeseburger and fat potato fries. A skinny frame has no place in the Arctic. Anywhere else this landscape would be winter.

After dinner I walk. I make note of things rendered immobile: The handlebars of a child's bicycle poke up out of sun-crusted snow. A rusted stove sleeps on its side. A snow machine with ripped seats lies half buried in a drift. Old tires, angled parts of three-wheelers, and the remains of boat motors mix a salvage pile in someone's front yard. All the sleeping parts and pieces of life in the Arctic reveal themselves as the stubborn snow begins its meltdown.

A burning wind scours the tundra and pulls me to the outer edges of town. At 10:30 p.m., the sun is at my back. The tundra reaches out into an endless sweep. Polar bear hides hang from drying racks on the beach. A cold lather of sea foam pounds the shoreline. I walk in search of the village cemetery, a frozen bone yard of the high Arctic.

Odd though it may be, I enjoy exploring places where the dead are housed. I peruse crosses and headstones, fascinated with the dates and ages of fellow travelers in the long and unbroken human line. People die away like cotton grass, and through the wear of time are forgotten. I had lost my father several years prior. Would I lose the memory of his easy-going gait and the sound of his soft-spoken voice?

Earlier a public safety officer, cruising the ice road in his heated pickup, warned me to stay within the village boundaries. Polar bears often wander the periphery searching for food, and I would make a marvelous meal. I knew of the bone pile a few miles from the village where unused portions of whale carcasses are deposited during the harvest, far enough away to discourage bears from getting too close to humans. But with the accelerated melting of the Arctic Ocean sea ice, polar bears were getting braver, venturing farther into town to feed.

The officer joked about the foolish *tanik*, who, on their visits to the village, walk the ice-slicked roads at 20 below (what in God's name for?), or worse, the runners who race around town scantily clad in spandex running suits. "Crazy white people who get their asses in trouble," he said. His people know better than to romanticize the landscape.

The ground breathes in icy swirls at my feet, like smoke struggling to rise. Fine snow fills the creases of my parka. The pounding wind shows no mercy. I keep walking. The ruff of my parka insulates my face from the cold. Swallowed in my hood, only *I* can hear myself speak.

Scattered on a barren patch of tundra, driftwood crosses emerge from the snow. Two bleached whalebone ribs spike up from a drift, marking an old whaling captain's grave. I walk along the row of graves and whisper the names and dates of those departed. I imagine a father talking to his dead son through a curtain of tears. Or a wife angry with her husband for leaving their family confused and alone.

In spirit we are never alone; we crave to talk to our dead. We need them though they don't need us. By speaking to them, we remember. Would I someday forget my father?

His burial was held on a cold March day in a Michigan suburb. As we rode in the limo to the gravesite, my brothers paraded a line of off-the-cuff remarks that had us laughing out loud, puns that were a steady trademark of my dad's lexicon. Punch lines kept coming (even Mother laughed) until we noticed the straight line on the lips of the limousine driver, who glanced back at us aghast. What could he possibly be thinking? We were a family, a little less whole but still unbroken after losing our most precious member.

The wind blew sideways in severe gusts, when only hours earlier the sun shined. Shoots of green grass became weighted with a miserable wet snow. I was led to sit down with my mother and sister in the front row graveside, and we huddled, pulling our skirts down over our knees, shoving our hands into deep coat pockets. Someone placed a blanket over our shivering legs.

A cousin leaned forward from behind. "Complete conspiracy, this weather," he said. "Isn't it just like Uncle Bob to give us hell?"

A smile leaked across our somber faces and one of Dad's lines flitted up in my mind. *Weather's so damn bad even the birds are walking.*

Managing medications is like throwing darts at a moving target. Sometimes we get it right, but often we miss the mark. We fumbled with a mix of pills: one for pain, one for aggression, and one for sleeping. The medication to reduce agitation was simply not working, as evidenced by the doctor firsthand. During one appointment, I watched my father's agitation escalate when the doctor's attention was placed solely on me, as if my father were not present. Like he was an old book with yellowed pages, shelved in the back of the room.

Stop swimming, the doctor said. Stop playing golf. Stop driving. Angry that his last strand of independence was being stripped away, my father raised his cane and struck, smacking the wall just inches above the doctor's head.

Now he watched me from the living room, between parted curtains as I cleaned out his car in the driveway. "Dad, I agree with the doctor. You can't drive anymore," I said. I spilled the contents of his glove compartment onto the kitchen table. He looked at me meanly and tried to spit but his effort fell short.

"So, *you're* one of them now too, huh?" he said. A string of drool hung from his bottom lip.

"It will be okay if he has back surgery," my mother said. "He's just in too much pain."

His daily crying and moaning spells lasted hours. Was it physical pain (he had had intermittent back pain for years) or was it psychic pain? Or both? Witnessing another small part of his life fall away while unable to do anything about it was bleak and insufferable.

"This isn't pain, Mother. It's infarction dementia," I said. "People in pain suffer, but they don't strike others."

"What the hell do *you* know?" she yelled, her fist delivering a hard blow to the table. I looked at her in alarm. I'd never before heard her speak in an angry, contemptuous way. It was more like her to speak softly, to acquiesce.

"You have *no idea* what constant pain can force a person to do," she said. Her conviction was understandable, and I knew she was right. I hid my father's keys and placed an ad in the paper.

Desperate spells of whining and crying continued, amplified by indignant behaviors. One morning my father tore through the bedroom closet stripping hangers bare. He heaped all his clothes on the living room floor and flung boots from the hallway closet on top of the pile. "There," he said, hands on his hips, "I'm going *home* soon."

It was painful witnessing his losses as every shred of meaning sloughed off like dry skin. My father was losing ground, and there was nothing we could do but catch him whenever and wherever he fell. It was our task to make him comfortable, ease his pain. Dispense love and dignity as best we could.

My attention fell to Mother. Her petite, five-foot-four-inch frame had lost 25 pounds. Dark circles were carved under her eyes. She hung onto a semblance of normalcy by a thinning frayed rope. She didn't sleep at night because he didn't sleep at night. As everything in his life fell away, so did everything in hers. All my silent prayers went to her, to give her strength, to let her live the rest of her days in peace. It was too late to set limits to his child-like behaviors, actions that were caused by the faulty pathology of his brain. Now there was no going back.

Vascular dementia is caused by reduced blood flow to the brain, usually as a result of a series of mini strokes. My father's brain craved oxygen-rich blood, but the highway to its destination petered out at the level of the carotid artery. His sensibilities dwindled like candle wax, dripping away slowly with each new insult.

During the first few months of decline he floated in and out of lucidity, at times talking gibberish and at other times speaking with full intelligibility. He remembered close relatives, picked up the mail each day and took enjoyment in helping my mother with household tasks, like washing dishes and dusting. Helping out was a positive mood change that gave us hope. We clung to inklings of small tangible changes though later learned this sudden "helpfulness" was a typical characteristic of dementia.

One afternoon after a visit to a relative's home and too much stimulation around the dinner table, my father took a turn for the worse. He couldn't stay awake during the visit and napped most of the day. On the hour-long drive home, he sat in the passenger seat and I drove, with Mother comfortably seated in the back. We were discussing the pleasant meal we'd shared when, out of the blue, he grabbed a hold of the seatbelt and clawed it away from his chest in a desperate attempt to break free. "You don't love me anymore," he shouted. "You're laughing at me." His agitation escalated. "You never loved me."

Frightened I pulled over to the side of the road. His face reddened as he spewed assaults of past wrongs aimed solely at my mother, accusations derived from misperceptions and an active imagination. He flailed his arms without directly striking me, and I felt lost on what to do next, how best to help him. All I could do was wait. Not retaliate. Guide him gently into the back seat. Once settled next to my mother, he calmed down. She held his hand firmly in her lap. "I'm sorry," he sobbed. "I'm so very sorry."

His reddened cheeks were wet with tears. Not maudlin tears but clean and honest expressions of regret. Oddly, during his decline, when he had everything to lose, a new tenderness sprang forth. Gestures of handholding and touching, difficult to openly express in his younger years, were demonstrated toward my mother with ease. Pent-up emotions over the course of a lifetime rose to the surface. In the midst of fear and confusion, he stumbled on personal revelations. He could say in all earnestness *I'm sorry* and *I love you*.

Writer Virginia Woolf spoke of an inner dignity we all possess, an impenetrable part of our selves that can never be reached, even though we live closely with our spouses for decades. The deepest parts of ourselves are well hidden and often the last treasures we are impelled to unearth. Poets, with their wellspring of honesty, have always told us this.

How we make a living, our relationships with family and friends, what gains us notice or credit—none of these touch the center of ourselves. No matter how close we grow to people around us, they can't ever really know our "resolute innerness." We are born alone and we die alone. That glint of selfhood we can't share with others may become illuminated *when we're forced, at moments of exposure* to reveal it, however brief and surprising it may be.

A closer intimacy and warmth developed between my parents during their most difficult time. Heaven knows they loved each other deeply.

Caring daily for my father morphed into a manageable routine until a more serious disturbance woke us from our beds. The slamming of distant doors at 2:00 a.m. found us rushing around in a panic. Standing in his pajamas at the complex's swimming pool, staring down into the water, my father was toeing the edge of his own life and death. We'd spent many summers on the beaches of Lake Michigan, our confidence in learning to swim a direct result of his joy at being so at ease in the water. Where had his disordered thinking taken him now? Was he going to jump in?

I shook with fear as I took hold of his arm and led him away from the pool. We stumbled up the small flight of stairs and back into the apartment. Weak and wrung out from crying, he laid down without a struggle.

"Why are you doing this to me?" his misplaced pleas growing.

Trembling, I bent down and kissed his forehead. Mother patted the blanket under his chin. We both acknowledged we'd just weathered a dangerous close call.

"Why?" he continued. "Why?"

Mother, looking gray and defeated, lowered herself into a chair. I approached the subject of nursing home care, a conversation we'd had before. Giving him up to institutional care was cruel abandonment in her mind. She regarded this option as a sentencing that would anger him beyond measure, an action she thought he would deem unforgiveable. I had no doubt she'd sacrifice her own life to look after him.

One night while my mother slept (a miracle in itself), my father attempted to watch his favorite TV program. He flipped through channels. Cursed. Flipped some more. Once he hit the mark, he couldn't follow the speaker's voice, didn't understand the storyline. His frustration mounted. The program was too loud. Or it was too soft. He rose from his chair and shuffled toward me in the kitchen. Under his breath he mumbled a long string of nonsensical language. Then as if to wake up the world and all the sleeping people in it he shouted clearly, "I'm gonna die soon!"

"Right?" He jutted out his chin, challenging me. "Right? Tell me. I'm dying, right?" He stepped forward, dropped his cane to the floor and fell into my open arms. We cried together and then I offered, "Yes, Dad, you are." I couldn't pretend or hide from him the truth.

Later I thought my father would have found it funny had I told him, at a healthier time, a story about my son. When my oldest son was six, he tried to understand the mystery of death. He laid down on the couch with a small pillow under his head, closed his eyes, and forced his arms and legs still. He tried calming his body, stiff as he could make it, every twitch and flutter controlled. He opened his eyes and closed them again, waiting for something to happen. But his sweet breath kept rising and falling through no will of his own. He shot up from the couch. "Mom, I can't do it. I just *can't* be dead."

And that was that.

My father lasted less than a year in private nursing home care. After he died, my mother, in her stoic devotion, visited each of her children from Texas to Alaska and back to Michigan, returning home to die the following year. She predicted her time of death, almost willed it, as though her life had been lived for him, and for us, exclusively.

His face was waxy, his thick wavy hair in perfect place at the open casket visitation. A suit and tie didn't describe him well, too formal. Pressed slacks and spit-shined shoes weren't him, too perfect if perfection was the goal. There was a smirk, like that foolish kid-like smile on his lips I so loved in life. Through his long fingers vined a string of black rosary beads joined by an ornate silver cross, like the one my devout grandmother clutched daily, mumbling prayers under her breath. The wrinkles in his face, the lines of struggle, were gone. He didn't look asleep or peaceful, just gone.

Where did you go, Dad, when your body turned cold? Your legs were tangled in nursing-home sheets while mother slept at home, alone. We didn't get a call until morning. My deepest sorrow was that we weren't there to hold his hand, to help carry him across the divide. I often wonder if he called for Mother or recited his children's names. I wonder what, if anything, would come next for him now that the final play was over. Will there be another *becoming* for him, or for any of us, after the winds of storms blow over?

I looked at him for a long time and I looked up above him, waiting for a sign or a message or *something* and I thought: Did a soul leave his body minutes after he took his last breath, or hours or days later? Where is my dad, now? Time chews up and swallows everything and everyone.

Sadness came in waves. The night of his funeral I slept in his place next to my mother and had a simple dream of walking alone on a dirt road, though my feet weren't touching the ground.

Over a century ago, the indigenous people of the Arctic understood the world from a shamanic tradition. All earthly things were imbued with spirit: tundra grass, stones, mountains, animals, water, and wind. The dominant religion of the Inupiat today is Christianity, though the divinity of the natural world still holds meaning. "Very well," an elder once said, "God made the earth, but Raven made it first."

Many northern people practice Christianity with a nuanced twist in regards to the journey of the soul. A soul doesn't leave the body immediately but is believed to wander the earth with the capacity to hurt living people unless it is assigned to a new person. A soul lives on in the newborn it is assigned to so that its roaming spirit has a new home. The child is seen as an incarnation of the ancestor. The ancestor's name-soul is within the child, keeping it safe and anchored to the earth.

In the Catholic tradition, humans have immortal souls that separate at the time of death and are judged *immediately*. Based on a person's good behaviors, he is ushered to either the holiness of heaven or the everlasting damnation of hell. I was sure, if there were such a thing, my dad would congregate with his brothers in heaven, palming a basketball in each hand or analyzing their backswings.

My father's "going home" ceremony played out in a traditional Catholic Mass. The god of Catholicism had left me decades ago, and nature was where I now worshipped, believing that when we die, like other plants and animals, our ashes feed the earth, springing into new sources of energy in the next cycle of birth. Father Tim didn't deliver a eulogy about my dad's life, his family, or his passions. Instead he preached a sermon about eternal life, and even though I don't believe in life after death (at least I don't think so), the priest's kind and loving words still brought comfort.

Slowly circling the casket Father Tim rocked an incense lantern as frankincense smoke curled and rose to heaven as the symbolic vehicle for my dad's recently departed soul. Breathing the incense, I was reminded of the things I loved most about the church as a child: the candle-lit midnight Mass at Christmas with its glorious hymns. How I kneeled next to my mother as she lit novena candles and prayed for the safety and well-being of her five children, an activity she engaged in weekly for over 40 years.

I remember in church my bowed head. Looking down at my dress, hands folded in my lap, my shiny patent-leather shoes perfectly aligned. My knees bruised from climbing trees. Looking up at my dad in his starched white shirt, his full attention on the priest delivering a sermon on applying God's word in our lives. How, through prayer, we can develop patience and forgiveness and love.

Further on we kneel for the Eucharistic prayer, where the body and blood of Christ are celebrated. "You are here to kneel where prayer has been valid," T. S. Eliot wrote. We kneel in thanks. We kneel to surrender to God's plan for us. We kneel to express bare reverence. And when it was time to kneel, I was all too often rebellious and lazy.

My stomach growled or a subtle pain would curve across my shoulders, and slyly I'd lower myself to the pew and sit. Ever so gently, my father would lay his hand on my lower back and urge me to my knees in a show of ceremonial respect. And if how we move our bodies reflects our state of mind, kneeling and standing and sitting tall were my father's preferred postures for his children.

In adulthood, miles and years away from the church and its teachings, I sit in a meditative lotus posture on a hardwood floor, not for mere minutes, but for hours. During these times, I often think of my dad's hand, urging me to sit up straight and lift my pleas to the heavens. Both gestures, I see now, are one in the same: a reaching out to the source of our comfort and practice. We sit and empty ourselves, pray for a peaceful state of mind. We kneel and try to understand the meaning of our problems and heartaches as we ask for compassion and guidance.

How does one navigate a whiteout when lost on the tundra? I asked this of an Inupiat hunter. He said you first look at the old snow, not the new drifts. Look for tails on the small hard clumps of old snow. The wind usually blows from the east in his region, so the tail is most likely on the west-northwest side of the clumps. With this scrap of information, you can compile a grid on the land and speculate the direction in which you are traveling.

How does one find her way after losing a loved one?

The evening before departing Kaktovik, I walk again to the cemetery to smell the brisk air, to practice death in advance perhaps, or to simply talk to my dad.

The cold wind catches my breath and brings tears to my eyes. For a moment, my imagination takes over as I recall the public safety officer's warning of hungry polar bears traveling the edges of town, looking for a meal. The wind drums the fabric of my parka. Slowly I scan from side to side. The drumming gets louder and for an instant, I freeze in my tracks.

I throw down my hood, spin around on my heels, and face the imminent danger, but there is none. No polar bear. I walk on. The wild wind caresses my face, and the cold sun travels by small degrees across the sky. In short bursts of solitude in times like this, I remember my dad the most, when the dissonance of everyday life quiets down.

At breakfast the next morning, an elder tells me a story about a hunter who had died on a late summer day many years prior, in that short window of time when the ice had finally melted. They had nowhere to keep the body fresh for the scheduled viewing and service a few days later. Out of necessity, the body was placed in a walk-in freezer at the village school. A new teacher starting her assignment in August opened the freezer door and nearly passed out from fright.

"Typical bureaucrats, the health board flew in from Anchorage with their clipboards and worried faces," he says. "They performed their evaluation and decided not to cite the village for a bad meat violation."

He says this with a straight face, eyebrows lifted, pulling me into the joke, or is it a joke? I really can't tell. It sounds like something my dad would say, the way he'd throw out a line and reel me in. Death is morose and sad and ironically kind of funny too.

"Now we have a vaulted locker, a mini morgue of sorts," he adds. "Holds a body till the ground thaws. If it ever truly does this far north."

In a way, I knew my father better through the days of his death than the days of his life. What I witnessed at the end were his truest sorrows. I could feel the fear and despair carved into the lines of his face, the setting of his jaw, the way his eyes spelled the story of defeat. These are the greatest struggles of a lifetime for all of us.

At the center of my father's greatest suffering, I witnessed his greatest capacity for intimacy, where he emanated a love unfiltered with conditions or commandments. Nearing the end, he looked at me like he did when I was a child. When I was eight and we followed a trail through golden beach grass on the shores of Lake Michigan. Our heads tipped back and laughing, we watched the smooth unfurling of pillow clouds, and I felt safe. Loved. My hand so small in his.

COPPER HOUSE

The happiness of the drop is to die in the river.
Al Ghazali

How we walked the gray silt road
Sitka roses pricking our ankles
rock-flour dusting the bowed heads of bluebells

How angled black spruce towered
over needled tundra, quivering
in the balance

How we dowsed the ground, probing
the earth's current with a rusty wire, looking
for water, minerals, the energy of stones

The land spoke, told
us exactly where to build,
another ten degrees east, downriver
facing the morning sun and dense green hills

How in my dream
standing in line with the others

I stepped up to the mirror when it was my turn
and faced a blinding circle of light

My only task to turn my head
just a notch, so that my eyes
would hook into the ringed aura and

There would lie a faith, unshattered

the assurance of things hoped for, the conviction of things not seen
faith that would move mountains and cast them out to sea

How the river roared down like thunder
tearing roots, grinding trees

Cleaving stone, how brown water
devoured solid ground, and

how my faith, light as stone dust

dried up in the flood

It's ceremonial, the ritual I follow each time I visit our cabin, a place we call Copper House. High up on a bank it overlooks the muddy brown waters of the Copper River. Before I unload the car, before I turn propane tank knobs, before I haul water, there is another priority. I walk the river's edge to observe its curious mood. How slow or fast is it moving, how deep and how shallow its route? It churns out a melody that soars high and low and often changes tune by the hour.

The trees thirst but with shallow roots. The god of erosion is worshipped here. I calculate how close the water is eating its way toward the cabin. How much time until the next big mud stream carves a new path in the shelf below. I zero in on the oldest spruce in the pack that barks its age in an ever-widening circumference, 200 years maybe? It is still standing though it wobbles and creaks in the wind, barely teetering on the edge of collapse.

One can perceive the river's liberated ways differently, of course, on any given day. It may be a nuisance and threat to owners whose homes and cabins perch precariously on its fragile bank; or, to seasoned rafters it may be an exciting, challenging ride. I hope for a steady and predictable pace of erosion, though the river's intentions have nothing to do with my unscientific calculations. It pays no mind to my human pleas.

The tang of river smell and churning damp earth mixes with the aroma of fresh ground coffee rising from my cup. We sit on stumps with friends, high up on the bank, and watch the spectacle of moving water. The river is a lot like fire. You can't take your eyes off it. Your vision lingers there in a soft lull, and you savor the soothing sounds of its constant motion. Across its wide expanse, willows shoot their wands upward, and beyond their spearing branches, black spruce and birch cloak the hills. And if that is not enough, far off and away, a young volcano named Mount Drum, capped by a lid of snow, paints the clouds pink.

Nick, the old homesteader who sold us the riverfront property, moved dirt and boulders decades ago, with the intention of slowing down the river's mad rush along his land. On the banks of the river in the Athabascan village of Tazlina, he took matters into his own hands as many a pioneer did in those days. He excavated tons of dirt and rock, creating a spit in the river, a jut of land to prevent massive erosion of the ground downriver. His man-made protrusion held steadfast for over 50 years. The rock structure created a fast-moving rapid and a big drop that rafters loved to shoot through, putting on a show for those of us watching from the bank.

But fast-moving water has a history of reclamation, no matter how hard we construct barriers to hold it back, no matter how hard we try to contain its power. Moving water dismantles everything in its path. It strips the ground of its clothing and never looks back on the chaos left behind.

Second only to the Yukon in silt load, the Copper River is one of the fastest, most rugged rivers in Alaska. Its 300-mile stretch covers ground that serpentines through the Wrangell and Chugach Mountains, fed by melting glaciers at its headwaters. The Copper Glacier, atop Mount Wrangell, is the ringmaster. When the sun melts glacier ice slowly in the spring, the flow of water is somewhat predictable though no one is ever 100 percent sure what will happen. Most years the Copper rises and levels off, eating away bank that's hardly noticeable. Other years when the sun beats fast and hard, so fast that alpine lakes are filled to the brim, water from the melting glacier gushes down the mountain, creating havoc that's impossible to predict.

A testimony to the unrelenting power of the river is told by a friend who experienced first-hand the river's uncontrollable tantrums. He and his buddies were rafting a section of the river that carves its way in front of Childs Glacier. Without warning, car-sized icebergs calved into the river, displacing their boat and its contents several hundred feet from the middle of the current. They held tight their boat as the wave action tossed them up onto solid ground. Spawning salmon were flung out of the water and landed in the branches of trees. River debris, drift logs, errant paddles (rendered useless) and the shocked looks on the boaters' faces all washed up together and came to rest on what was, only moments before, dry forested ground.

We built our cabin up high on a bank along a slow, lazy bend in the river. We worked steadily through all the seasons using portable generators to power our tools. We poured a cement foundation. We put up walls and negotiated scaffolding. Board by board and inch by inch, the building was painstakingly constructed with plenty of shared sweat equity.

Plowing through plans, we mulled over decisions on a septic system versus an outhouse and settled on a composting toilet. Fueled by attractive building ideas, we installed windows that brought the river in view. Over a five-year period, we paid for its construction out of pocket and employed the help of generous friends who contributed their labors and laughs.

In the four years following completion, we lost a total of nine feet of soil. When heavy rains weakened the ground, the shallow roots of century-old spruce trees popped out of the earth. Little more than a good gust and the trees toppled into the muddy current. Our engineering friends piped in on how to remedy the situation and save our land, but in the end, the earth will have her final say. We were not trying to fool Mother Nature, just keep her at bay.

We listened to good advice from people who live along these rivers, the Athabascans who have been fishing the Copper for centuries. Add rocks along the bank at mean high water mark, they said. Place the rock bed at a sharp angle facing upriver, forcing the water to curl around it so the flow becomes slow and still near the bank. Engineer friends suggested using rip-rap and gabions to hold back the surge. Begin by piling boulders in and as they sink to scour depth, add more. We considered all our options. One curious onlooker who stopped by while we worked dismissed our plans altogether. "You have nothing to worry about," he said. "This river is nowhere near the next 100-year flood."

Nowhere, near.

The Copper House remained prone to being whisked off its foundation and launched into sludge brown waters, where it would heave itself into the tributaries that merge with other streams and rivers. Finally, it would be set free at sea and ride the ocean currents with all our cherished memories and labors sculpted deep within its walls.

"Thar' she blows," I wrote in our guest book. Attempting to stay light about the situation, I joked about "the bank that ain't," knowing if our efforts failed we'd have to move the entire structure, and at a huge expense. We remained on constant watch and moved forward with our plans to buy time. The days slipped away. We secured large rocks from a pit nearby and added them to a spit of our own creation at an angle upriver. Just as we were advised, our efforts successfully slowed the frantic rush of water.

Not for long, though. On the morning of May 30 water flowed 10 feet from the cabin. On May 31 water flowed five feet from the northeast corner. Trees leaned over and toppled. The ground cracked beneath our feet, and yards of bank sloughed off into the current.

The fire pit disappeared. Knowing its sentimental value, a friend leaned over a tree and grabbed the giant bird feeder I gave my husband on our first Christmas at the cabin. Then the massive tree holding the bird feeder was ripped from the ground and bounced downriver in the current.

The river barreled on and reclaimed its old route, a flow that carved a wide path into the land well over a hundred years ago. The bench of land below the 20-foot bank in front of the cabin was gone. In a matter of hours, the gravel road that led to the fish wheel disappeared and our cozy bend in the river morphed into a long straight line. The jumble of boulders bulldozed in place over 50 years ago lasted no longer. They were either pushed downriver or covered over in the heavy flow of water.

A late-night discussion on what would be our next course of action issued a bundle of questions: should we empty the cabin of all our belongings, futon beds, a propane woodstove, could we salvage the windows? The stove, refrigerator, clothing, an environmental toilet system housed below in the crawlspace, a 300-gallon water tank? Should we empty and save what we could or attempt to move the whole building a couple football fields away from the disappearing bank?

Through all of this nail biting, strategizing the next logical step, I suddenly felt a complete calm wash over me. The situation was clearly out of our hands. Our attempts at saving would either work or not. An orange Super Cub flew low over the river and tipped its wing our way. The pilot waved. He was examining the damage up and down river, probably shaking his head over all our improvements that were so haphazardly ripped away. But our troubles paled in comparison to our neighbors'.

Flood watches were put in place. Everyone was watching the rivers: pilots, ground observers, forecasters, and villagers. We all needed to be prepared to react. Our only mistake was waiting too long. We should have started talking about and planning for what we would do should the volume of water soak the ground and suck the Copper House right out from under our feet.

Villagers along the Yukon River knew real suffering. In the village of Galena, 90 percent of the homes were damaged by floodwaters. The ice jam causing the flooding was caught in a 180-degree turn at a place called Bishop Rock. Like sewage caught in the crook of a pipe, sheets of ice stopped up the turn and the water dammed for 30 miles upriver. Once the ice broke free, all hell broke loose.

Over 200 villagers fled to Fairbanks, while others stayed and took refuge in a makeshift shelter at the village school. Emergency sirens, customarily used to alert people to fires, crowded the afternoon sky. One villager spent the night in his boat as seven feet of water filled his home, lifting it off its foundation. Airstrips were covered in water preventing planes from landing.

And it wasn't just the Yukon; the flow of many major rivers was held back by ever-growing mounds of sheet ice. The Kuskokwim and Koyukuk resisted the urge to give birth, until the last minute when an explosion of water gushed through towns, sweeping away everything not nailed down. Unless you lived inland, you didn't escape the floods.

We were safe from the river's clutch, though just by the seat of our pants. We contacted movers who were so busy saving other structures, their only offering was to schedule us three weeks out. We no longer had three weeks, or even three days.

In a last-ditch effort, I contacted a construction company working in a nearby village. The crew, who had been working around the clock, could come in two days, provided the cabin was still standing when they arrived.

Through sheer luck our fate was sealed. The Copper House and all its contents, saved. Twelve hours before the move, I dug up half a dozen sturdy spruce trees to replant afterward, heartsick that so many healthy trees had to be uprooted to make room for the move. Still, I was thankful we made it and hoped the trees in their new location would too.

I've added a new activity to my ritual of examining the behavior of the river. I now peruse my fledgling trees that declare *hey, old man river we're here to stay,* as they resist the perilous tug of the water's reach.

Our old homesteader friend has since died, and I think he would be surprised by the new shape the river has taken. An aerial view would show lazy turns and deeply etched bends transformed into a long straight line like the hem on a dress. Where the water was once deep and fast, it now wears shallow riffles where a rafter would have to spring from his boat and portage his heavy load. Or if he chose, he could picnic on an island of black sand, a new beach that appears to have erupted out of nowhere.

We should have listened to the ancestors. *Dena nena henash*, they say in Athabascan. "The land speaks." If only we had listened.

Fall arrives several months after the move. My husband is off with his friend Stone on a trip to Delta for the fall caribou hunt. Alone for a week, I finish grouting a mosaic of a sockeye salmon with glossy red and silver stones that will hang over the front door.

I view the yard from the front window. Silt that passes for soil has grown new weeds, and the blooming of wild pink roses carries on unfazed by the soil's new configuration.

There are always those hardy ones, plants unperturbed by bitter cold, plants that grow in only a few hours of sun, plants that hold tenaciously to the ground that birthed them. How does life spring forth so soon after an upset? How does *anything* grow in weightless gray dust, silt you can't clump in your hands?

Hard sounds batter the roof and, like fuses blowing, rain patters the ground in big thick drops. I think of slippage; how everything we try and nail down shifts and sinks yet so quickly bounds forth to its former shape or creates a new shape that's equally resilient. A thunderclap sounds as a twist of black clouds thickens. Our dog scares easily and pops up from a restful curl on his bed. He trots over to me and lies down close.

Across the river, a lone wolf scratches at the ground. It startles me to see it, so lean and black, unprotected in the rain. In an instant it looks up, sniffs the air, swivels its head, and is gone. I wonder if I'd seen it at all, or was it just a trace of something else?

The night enters quickly, with no stars or moon in the sky. Darkness falls all around and there is just me and the dog and the sucking black river. I sit in the dark and choose gratitude as my prayer.

The following April we carry our lawn chairs down to the river. We step over blowdown that occurred the night before in a windstorm. Rabbit scat peppers the ground where downed branches lie gnawed, stripped of bark in long smooth patches. We carry out our ritual once again, to watch the river's crazy ways.

A large shelf of ice breaks loose and careens like an enormous barge in the current. Ice cakes of all sizes and shapes spin and smash into each other. The serendipitous bouncing and shape-shifting of the cakes is a curiosity, an entertainment of sorts. We drink a few beers and watch the show.

Breakup finally fizzles out. The sun warms the ice, slowly. No jams or flooding are headed our way. Relief. Yet we stay on river watch, always. We predict how next year's salmon run will turn out, in light of the river's drastic change in shape and speed. We construct what-if scenarios now that we have some experience under our belts. If the gravel bar out front disappears, the fish will swim through much closer to the bank. They smell the deep holes where the water is colder. Someone notes a change upriver, how a new set of islands has formed in the blink of an eye.

But the main reason we watch the river with the patience and persistence of a weed growing up through concrete is because we are simply unable to take our eyes off its breathing, leaping energy.

The river doesn't follow a straight line, pulled
by the moon but roams
like a wolf following root, skin, and scent.
Ice jams push sludge-brown waters
(on a screaming path), uprooting centuries-old trees and
cutting the silt bank to its knees.

We count our blessings
shore up with big rocks, muscle against the inevitable,
learn to soften and adapt.

A fish pulled from the net slides through my slippery hands,
ravens soar, the sky goes rust and
everything, it seems
Is carved in sand.

This is the year of records, they say of 2013. This may have been the most extensive flooding I've seen in all my life, the most damaging in any local's living memory. But like laws, records are made to be broken.

The signature of the river tells us this: the only sure constant is change, and that is where we place our faith. Faith the rain will soften the earth and the trees will loosen and fall. Faith the silt will blow like flour unable to hold a core. Faith the high-water mark will stay for days, maybe even for weeks. Not because of arbitrary punishments or rewards.

But because rivers will do what rivers do.

BIBLIOGRAPHY

Abram, David. *Becoming Animal, An Earthly Cosmology.* New York: Pantheon Books, 2010.

Achebe, Chinua. *Things Fall Apart.* New York: Penguin, 1994.

Barker, James H., Ann Fienup-Riordan, and Theresa Arevgaq John. *Yupiit Yuraryarais: Yup'ik Ways of Dancing.* Fairbanks: University of Alaska Press, 2010.

Beisner, Beatrix, Christian Messier, and Luc-Alain Giraldeau, eds. *Nature All Around Us: A Guide to Urban Ecology.* Chicago: University of Chicago Press, 2012.

Berman, Morris. *Wandering God: A Study in Nomadic Spirituality.* Albany: State University of New York Press, 2000.

Burch, Ernest S. "The Inupiat and the Christianization of Arctic Alaska," *Études/Inuit/Studies.* 18, no. 1–2 (1994).

Dean Moore, Kathleen, Kurt Peters, Ted Jojola, and Amber Lacy, eds. *How It Is: The Native American Philosophy of V. F. Cordova.* Tucson: University of Arizona Press, 2007.

Fienup-Riordan, Ann. *Eskimo Essays.* New Brunswick, NJ: Rutgers University Press, 1990.

———. *The Living Tradition of Yup'ik Masks: Agayuliyararput (Our Way of Making Prayer).* Seattle: University of Washington Press, 1996.

———. *Wise Words of the Yup'ik People: We Talk to You Because We Love You.* Lincoln: University of Nebraska Press, 2005.

Freeman, Milton M. R., ed. *Endangered Peoples of the Arctic: Struggles to Survive and Thrive.* Westport, CT: Greenwood Press, 2000.

Geeting, Doug, and Steve Woerner. *Mountain Flying.* New York: Tab Practical Flying Series, 1988.

Harrison, K. David. *When Languages Die: The Extinction of the World's Languages and the Erosion of Human Knowledge.* Oxford: Oxford University Press, 2008.

House, Freeman. *Totem Salmon: Life Lessons from Another Species.* Boston: Beacon Press, 1999.

John, Theresa Arevgaq. M.A. "Yuraryararput Kangiit-Lu: Our Ways of Dance and Their Meanings." Ph.D. diss., University of Alaska, Fairbanks, 2010.

Kawagley, Angayuqaq Oscar. *A Yupiaq Worldview: A Pathway to Ecology and Spirit.* Long Grove, IL: Waveland Press, 2006.

Kohanav, Linda. *The Tao of Equus: A Woman's Journey of Healing and Transformation through the Way of the Horse.* Novato, CA: New World Library, 2001.

Krauss, Michael. *Alaska Native Languages: Past, Present, and Future.* Fairbanks: Alaska Native Language Center, 1980.

Lee, Molly C., ed. *Not Just a Pretty Face: Dolls and Human Figurines in Alaska Native Cultures.* Fairbanks: University of Alaska Press, 2006.

Lipka, Jerry, Gerald Vincent, and the Ciulistet group. *Transforming the Culture of Schools, Yup'ik Eskimo Examples.* Mahwah, NJ: Lawrence Eerlbaum Associates, 1998.

Lynge, Finn. *Arctic Wars, Animal Rights, Endangered Peoples.* Hanover, NH: Dartmouth College: University Press of New England, 1992.

MacDonald, John. *The Arctic Sky: Inuit Astronomy, Star Lore, and Legends.* Iqaulit, NWT: Royal Ontario Museum/Nunavut Research Institute, 1998.

McClanahan, Alexandra J. *Growing Up Native in Alaska: Finding the Path to Identity.* Anchorage: CIRI Foundation, 2001.

Meade, Marie. "Sewing to Maintain the Past, Present, and Future." *Études/Inuit/Studies* 14, no. 1–2 (1990): 229–39.

———, transcribed and translated. *Yuliyararput, Our Way of Making Prayer, Yup'ik Masks and the Stories They Tell.* Edited by Ann Fienup-Riordan. Seattle: Anchorage Museum of History and Art in association with the University of Washington Press, 1996.

Merculieff, Ilarion, and Libby Roderick. *Stop Talking: Indigenous Ways of Teaching and Learning and Difficult Dialogues in Higher Education.* Anchorage: University of Alaska, 2000.

Murie, Margaret. *Two in the Far North.* Berkeley: Alaska Northwest Books, 1979.

Oleska, Michael, ed. *Alaska Missionary Spirituality.* New York: Paulist Press, 1987.

Oman, Lela Kiana. *Eskimo Legends*. Anchorage: Alaska Methodist University Press, 1975.

Orr, Eliza Cingarkaq, Ben Orr, Victor Kanrilak Jr., and Andy Charlie Jr. *Ellangellemni: When I Became Aware*. Fairbanks: Alaska Native Language Center, 1997.

Record, Holly. *A Case Study of Copper Center, Alaska*. Alaska OCS Socioeconomic Studies Program. Technical Report No. 7. Prepared for Peat, Marwick, Mitchell & Co. Contract No. AA550-CT6-61, 1979.

Roderick, Libby. *Alaska Native Cultures and Issues: Responses to Frequently Asked Questions*. Fairbanks: University of Alaska Press, 2010.

Spatz, Ronald, Jeane Breinig, and Patricia H. Partnow, eds. *Alaska Native Writers, Storytellers, and Orators: The Expanded Edition. Alaska Quarterly Review* 17, no. 3 and 4 (1999).

Spencer, R. F. *The North Alaskan Eskimo: A Study in Ecology and Society*. Bureau of American Ethnology Bulletin 171. Washington, D.C.: Smithsonian Institution, 1959.

Wilson, Jack. *Glacier Wings and Tails*. Anchorage: Great Northwest Publishing and Distributing Company, 1988.

ACKNOWLEDGMENTS

"On the Edge of Ice" first appeared in the literary journal *New Letters*, winning first place for creative nonfiction. It also appeared in *The Ultimate Thule: Journeys in Arctic Alaska, America's Northernmost Lands, a Web Anthology* edited by Shannon Huffman Polson.

"Water Mask" was previously published in *Cirque: A Literary Journal for the North Pacific Rim*.

"Women Taking Steam" first appeared in the anthology *Women Awakening: Discovering Our Personal Truths*, edited by Diane DeBella (Wild Ginger Press).

"Many Things Were Visible When the Earth Was Thin" first appeared in the literary journal *Stoneboat*.

An excerpt from "When Mountains Agitate the Wind" appeared in *Orion's* online venue titled "The Place Where You Live."

THANKS

A heartfelt *tsin'aen* to our Athabascan friends Arnold and Lucille Lincoln, who over the years metaphorically stood at the river's edge and helped us cross safely to the other side. Thank you for making your home ours. For the much-needed hot showers and homemade dinners, the late-night storytelling around your kitchen table, the times shared catching reds and harvesting them until our bones ached. For moving dirt, collecting stones, cutting trees, and so much more. Your labor and friendship buoyed my family well beyond measure and from those experiences, stories were born.

To my best friend and enduring partner, Kent Devine, who gently nudged me through every door of opportunity and swept clean any doubt in moving forward to fulfill my aspirations.

With gratitude for deep friendships. To Steve, captain extraordinaire, who safely navigated seas both big and small on our journey to Alaska. And to chef Julie for the dancing, singing, kayaking, good food, and laughter.

Thanks to Linda Hasselstrom, who facilitated initial edits, and to Andromeda Romano-Lax, who helped shape and order the manuscript with detailed care and attention. For reading and reviewing along the way, I thank J. Culkin, Debbie Clarke Moderow, Mary Kancewick, and Debby Dahl Edwardson. Your assistance was invaluable.

A special thank-you to Zachary, Christopher, and Kaylee Devine; to my siblings Christopher John Marzonie, Mark Marzonie, and Bethany Dixon for our shared lives filled with music and song. May our affections never be broken.

I could not have written this book without time spent in New Mexico, first at the Upaya Zen Center, followed by longer periods of concentrated writing time at the Casa del Sol on Ghost Ranch, where the late celebrated painter Georgia O'Keeffe lived an isolated artist's life. Every day I paid homage as I passed her historic adobe, with thanks for the creative life she inspired in me.

And lastly, I offer my devotion to the land. To the rugged contours of Alaska, and the enchanting high desert of New Mexico. It is within these magical places I feel most at home where strength, clarity, beauty, and a spiritual presence are felt and forever remembered.

MONICA DEVINE

Artist and writer Monica Devine has published work across several genres. "On the Edge of Ice" won first place for creative nonfiction with the literary journal *New Letters,* and her poem "No One Thing" was a first place winner in the Alaska State Poetry Contest. Additional writings and photographs have appeared in *Stoneboat, Cirque Journal, Alaska Magazine, Alaska Frontier Magazine, Children's Television Workshop,* and three anthologies. She has also authored five children's books, among them *Iditarod: The Greatest Win Ever,* a former nominee for the celebrated Golden Kite Award.

Monica studies figurative ceramics, photography, and writing from her home in Eagle River, Alaska. Her website Image, Sculpture, Verse can be viewed at monicadevine.com.